Beneath

These

Red

Cliffs

RONALD L. HOLT

Foreword by Floyd O'Neil

University of New Mexico Press
Albuquerque

BENEATH THESE RED CLIFFS

AN ETHNOHISTORY
OF THE UTAH PAIUTES

Library of Congress Cataloging–in–Publication Data
Holt, Ronald L., 1949–
Beneath these red cliffs : an ethnohistory of the Utah Paiutes /
Ronald L. Holt ; foreword by Floyd O'Neil.—1st ed.
p.   cm.
Includes bibliographical references and index.
ISBN 0–8263–1383–3
1. Paiute Indians—History—Sources.   2. Paiute Indians—
Government relations.   3. Paiute Indians—Social conditions.
4. Mormons—History—Sources.   5. Mormons—Social conditions.
I. Title.
E99.P2H65   1992
979.2'004974—dc20   92–13952
                                                        CIP

FIRST EDITION.

CONTENTS

ILLUSTRATIONS

TABLES

FOREWORD

IN THE HISTORY of the American Indians, a number of tribal groups have consistently been neglected by the scholarly community; among them are the Paiutes, and particularly the Paiutes who have dwelt in Utah. Theirs has been neither a happy history nor an experience of heroic conflict, but rather a chronicle of enervation and hopelessness, a story of the descent from a viable tribal life to one of economic dependency and despair.

In this volume Professor Ronald Holt makes a major contribution to the field of American Indian history and ethnography, by characterizing the Paiute experience with remarkable clarity. The work is meticulously well researched. Professor Holt has moved with great care and accuracy into the field of Mormon-Indian relations, but he has done so without dividing the intellectual landscape into Mormon and non-Mormon spheres. Better than any previous study, his work allows the evidence of history to dictate the conclusions.

There is, perhaps, no better place in the United States to examine the effects of paternalism than in Utah; that is even more true when one considers the nature of the Mormon-Indian relationship. The Paiutes were forced into "shantytowns" around southwestern Utah communities, where their level of life was marginal at best; but, astoundingly, they were among the tribes terminated from federal jurisdiction in the 1950s, in an act of utter irresponsibility by the federal government. This study treats that series of events in an objective manner, tracing the long process of the reabsorption of the group back into federal protection.

An interesting irony of this work is Professor Holt's description of the Paiutes' search for a scrap of land in the vast domain that was once their own. The dynamic of restoring a tribe as a ward of the federal government was not as simple as the passage of an act of Congress. The account of this attempt to recreate an operable tribal unit lays bare for the reader the power structure and the political forces in the modern rural West.

Professor Holt has accomplished the difficult feat of joining narrative and analysis; the result is a readable and engaging work.

Floyd A. O'Neil
DIRECTOR
American West Center
University of Utah

ACKNOWLEDGMENTS

I WOULD LIKE to acknowledge the help of numerous individuals, without whom this book would never have been completed. Dr. Floyd O'Neil, of the American West Center at the University of Utah, was always free with his time and his immense knowledge of Native American history. Dr. O'Neil also took time away from his busy schedule to write the foreword to this volume. Dr. Patricia Albers spent long hours reading the original manuscript that became my Ph.D. dissertation. Her comments, criticism, and support were invaluable. Attorney Mary Ellen Sloan and Dee Wilcox, of the BIA, allowed me to dig through their files and were generous with their time and expertise.

Numerous LDS officials and members spent long hours with me, discussing the historical and contemporary interaction of the Mormon church and the Paiutes. Special thanks to Omer C. Stewart, Allen Turner, John Boyden, Jr., and Parker Nielson. I am forever indebted to Elisa, Carol, Geno, Bob, Michael, and Greg for their help and support. The staff of the Denver Federal Records Center was very gracious and helpful. The Special Collections staff at both Southern Utah University and the University of Utah were also helpful hosts. My thanks to Mr. Brandon Hammons, who prepared the maps.

Finally I would like to thank the Utah Paiutes that took me into their homes and into their confidence. They have proved to be patient teachers and a continuing source of trust and encouragement. Any errors of interpretation, omission, or literary quality may be safely laid at my doorstep.

Ronald L. Holt
Weber State University
May 1991

INTRODUCTION

Life for the Paiutes is very hard. We suffer a lot. But I think in our hearts {gestures to chest} we are happier than the whites. We are happy because we know who we are. The young people—they are worse off. They can't talk Indian. They suffer and they don't know who they are . . . elderly Paiute, 1982

SUFFERING HAS NOT been a stranger to the Southern Paiutes of Utah. Over the past 150 years, they have been dispossessed of their lands, have suffered from hunger and cold, have died from untreated diseases, have been targeted by Mormon missionaries, have been terminated, and have been reinstated as a federally recognized tribe.

Their story is not only an epic of suffering, it is also a saga of triumphs, tenacity, and faith. They have met adversity with the easy dignity of a people confident in their ultimate fate. They abide and often thrive.

In this book, I have attempted to outline the history and culture of the Utah Paiutes through two major themes: dependency and paternalism. Dependency, or reliance on others, rests on an imbalance similar to that between parent and child. The fact that tribes might find themselves in situations of dependency was recognized in the 1950s:

Failure to maintain cultural and political independence often results in a reaction of defeatism which may be manifested in the neglect of ceremonial observances, the establishment of a dependency relationship with the dominant group, and population decline. (Social Science Research Council 1954:987)

Beginning in the 1960s, the model of "internal colonialism" as a means of explaining the dependent and exploited status of reservation-based Native Americans came into use.[1] Hagan gives a simple but powerful explanation of Native American dependency and underdevelopment:

> The essence of the colonial situation is that a people have been conquered, the functioning of its culture and social structure disrupted and suppressed in some degree, and an alien control imposed with such force that resistance is futile. By this definition the position of American Indian tribes is the archetype of colonialism, for their social structure and culture have been completely disrupted and suppressed more completely than those of any people conventionally referred to as colonial. (1961:471)

The concept of dependency shifts the concern away from viewing tribal populations as discrete, isolated groups and recognizes the importance of the weak structural position they occupy vis-à-vis the dominant power. Dominance may rest on military, economic, and/or political power. Dependency is a concept of relationships that are preconditioned by inequality.

The chains of dependency are often forged through patronage and strengthened by paternalistic assumptions. Goodell (1985:247) defines paternalism as "interference with others' autonomy justified by reasons referring exclusively to their welfare, good, happiness, needs, interests, or values. Thus paternalism is based on 'its ideological claim on benevolence.' "

Paternalism is usually legitimated by utilizing the asymmetrical power model of the parent-child relationship and mimicking the genuine concern of the parent, thereby hiding the conflictual basis of the ruler-subject relationship (Van den Berghe 1985). This line of thought leads Van den Berghe to conclude that paternalistic altruism is a form of parasitism in disguise.

Goodell (1985:250) hypothesizes a causal relationship between initiative (which presupposes a degree of autonomy) and corporate unity. Those who take the initiative may make decisions, suggest policies, or punish and reward through sanctions and gifts. A special kind of bond is, in turn, generated through these gifts; they create obligations to return other gifts or services (Mauss 1954:6–16). Thus a social bond is created. In a dependency situation, the beneficiary is unable to complete the cycle by offering a return gift. A person who cannot reciprocate loses status, prestige, and self-respect. In this framework the paternalist determines policy and maintains the initiative in the relationship with the beneficiary. The beneficiaries then react to policies generated by the paternalists and are sometimes allowed to administer or implement them. The beneficiaries, therefore, are never allowed to make the initial decisions that govern their lives and do not develop the abilities necessary for decisive autonomous action.

Paternalism is a consistent theme that governs the interaction of federal and Mormon church policy makers and the Paiutes. After the Anglo-Mormon occupation of their country, the Paiutes were isolated in small, "shantytown" enclaves adjacent to the Anglo settlements and were forced to define themselves through their dependent relationship to the Mormon church. By means of military superiority, the Mormons controlled the Paiutes by controlling access to their traditional means of production: food resources and water for irrigation. While the Mormons justified their dominance of the Paiutes through religious ideology, the foundations of this relationship rested on military superiority, and force was occasionally applied when ideology failed. The Mormons seized the social and political initiative as they seized the Paiutes' land; affairs that had previously been the responsibility of the Paiutes were referred to church officials and, later, to the BIA. The opinions or preferences of the Paiutes were seldom elicited and, when they were consulted, they were generally offered only a series of preconceived alternatives, one of which they were forced to accept.

The great irony of Paiute history is that, although the avowed purpose of both federal and Mormon policy was to make the Paiutes independent, the actual results of these policies have been to create and maintain a situation of insidious dependence on outside help. The paradoxical nature of this relationship is reminiscent of Goodell's (1985:248) statement that studies of paternalism have found "the negative consequence of 'being helped' as pervasive and profound as those of being exploited."

The Utah Paiutes were not only subjected to the tutelage of these missionary colonists, they were also neglected by the federal government and then ravaged by a series of ill-conceived and poorly administered federal policies.[2] The paternalistic policies of both the Mormon church and the United States government contributed to the creation and maintenance of poverty and frustration. The Paiute case provides us with a deeper understanding of the relationship between paternalism and colonialism and illustrates the dramatic effects of dependency on a conquered people. All these variables provide for a system of amplified feedback, in which the best-intentioned efforts of the state and religious bureaucracies have nurtured a condition diametrically opposite that of their stated intentions. Clearly one must decide whether, despite endless public announcements of actions taken for the good of the Indian, these policies were in fact well intentioned or whether they were self-serving, calculated attempts by both the church and federal bureaucracies to ensure the impotence of the Paiute Nation.

Beneath

These

Red

Cliffs

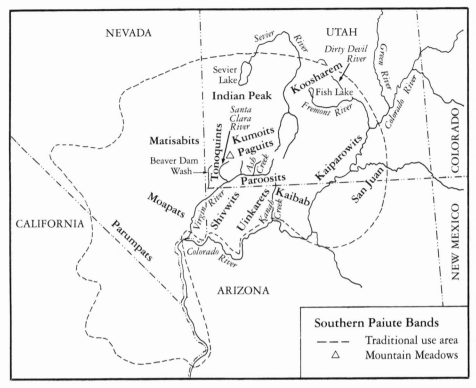

Figure 1. *The Southern Paiute Homeland*

1 OCCUPATION & DEPENDENCY

IN OCTOBER OF 1776, a party of Spanish explorers led by two Franciscans, Fray Francisco Domínguez and Fray Vélez de Escalante, ventured into the red-rock country of southern Utah. At Coal Creek near what is today Cedar City, Utah, they encountered about twenty Paiute women gathering seeds. This was the first recorded contact between Utah Paiutes and European explorers. The women were afraid of the strangers, and all but two were able to run away and avoid the explorers' questions.

The Utah Paiutes were characterized by the early explorers as a peaceful, somewhat timid society of foragers and horticulturalists. The primary mission of the Domínguez-Escalante expedition was to open an overland route between Santa Fe, New Mexico, and Monterey, California. The Spanish expedition failed in its overall goal of opening the way to Monterey, but it did open the eastern half of a route to the sea. This track came to be called the Old Spanish Trail.

Although the Spanish failed to follow up the Domínguez-Escalante venture and colonize Utah, slave traders and trappers traveled the Trail through Paiute lands. While these transients left their mark on the land, the Paiutes remained in control of their country. In the 1850s, however, with the arrival of colonists from the Church of Jesus Christ of Latter-Day Saints (LDS, or Mormons), the Paiutes were rapidly alienated from their land base. Less than one hundred years after Domínguez and Escalante's visit, the Paiutes were a destitute people who survived by begging and by doing seasonal and part-time work for the now dominant Anglo-Mormon settlers.

The Protohistoric Paiutes

The Southern Paiute language is one of the northern Numic branches of the large Uto-Aztecan language family. Southern Paiute, while varying in dialect from band to band, is very close to that of both the Southern and Northern Utes (Miller 1986:98–102).[1] Most scholars agree that Numic-speakers began a fanlike expansion throughout the Great Basin about 1000 A.D. (Lamb 1958:99, Madsen 1975:82–184, Bettinger and Baumhoff 1982). Madsen (1975:84) suggests that Paiute-Shoshone groups reached southwest Utah by 1100–1200 A.D.

In early historic times, Southern Paiutes lived in what became southern California, southern Nevada, southern Utah, and northern Arizona. The two largest population concentrations were along the Muddy River, in Nevada, and the Santa Clara River, in Utah.

The Paiutes are a short, stocky people. A Havasupai informant of Leslie Spier described the Paiutes of ca. 1859 in this manner:

> The men had bare bodies, breechclouts, but no leggings. The women wore only rabbitskin blankets on their bodies, tied over the right shoulder and down the right side; for skirts they wore doeskins with the hair left on; some wore skirts of mountain sheep skin with the hair on. The skirts came down to their knees and hung even all around. All wore sandals of soapweed, which extended up around the foot only a little way. The women wore conical basket hats; the men had headbands of soapweed; some had their hair in a knot tied with yucca strong [sic]. (Euler 1966:70)

The harsh environment of the Great Basin is often stressed in discussions of the Southern Paiutes; however, most Utah Paiutes lived adjacent to the Basin, on the Colorado Plateau, where resources were more readily obtainable. While the climatic variation of southern Utah posed problems for the Paiutes, it also offered them varied ecological zones to exploit and a more comfortable life, attainable by moving vertically at different seasons of the year.[2] Many Paiutes followed a pattern of seminomadic mobility, with base camps established in protected wintering areas, while other groups were based in cultivated riverine areas. Riverine groups also exploited seasonally available wild resources, in addition to their horticultural products. The territorial districts of the different Paiute groups were usually bounded by prominent geographic features, such as ridgelines, mountains, sinkholes, buttes, or washes (Palmer 1933). Reliable sources of water were important factors in the location of Paiute dwellings. For shelter the Paiutes traditionally utilized windbreaks, brush shelters, and more substantial winter dwellings made of juniper or aspen posts with wild ryegrass as filler, held in place by bark and/or willow boughs. Some winter houses were slightly excavated pithouses. Kelly (1964:158) notes that the Paiutes made use of the sweathouse, and that some of her informants attributed it to Navajo influences.

Subsistence

The Southern Paiutes of Utah, Arizona, and Nevada practiced a wide-spectrum approach to the utilization of their homeland. Prior to extensive white contact, the Southern Paiutes were a foraging people, with a marginal dependence on horticulture. Mobility was crucial in order for the people effectively to utilize the varied environments offered by the Colorado Plateau. To ensure this mobility, they constructed few elaborate tools or other items of a complex nature, although they did utilize a highly developed basketry complex, which served their needs in processing and transporting both wild and cultivated plant foods. Paiute campsites were generally located "at the base of a scarp or on its lower slopes, adjacent to water and to juniper stands" (Kelly 1964:55). Winter camps were located either at sheltered lower-elevation sites or at higher elevations near caches of pine nuts and plenty of fuel (Kelly and Fowler 1986:371). Thus not only did they take advantage of the various faunal and floral resources available during different seasons of the year, they also exploited the various elevations throughout their territory. The available data indicate that they followed a seasonal round of foraging and that some groups also integrated cultivating into their cycle (see table 1).

The Domínguez-Escalante journal (Warner 1976:79) mentions that Paiutes along Ash Creek were raising maize and irrigating their crops

Table 1. *Southern Paiute Composite Seasonal Round*

Season	Activities and Resources
Winter	A time of near starvation; agave; cacti; juniper berries and stored foods (utilize lowland resources).
Spring	Mescal; roots (*Peteria* and *Tsii*); rabbits; fish during spawning at Fish Lake; prepare and plant fields.
Summer	Plant fields; gather seeds (ricegrass) and roots such as "wild potatoes"; high-plateau berries; hunt mountain sheep, woodchuck and porcupine; fish at Fish Lake.
Fall	Harvest fields; communally hunt deer, antelope, and rabbits; gather *Artemisia* seeds, willow for baskets, and pine nuts; yucca; time to cache foods such as pine nuts.

with "well-dug irrigation ditches." During the 1840s virtually every traveler's diary mentioned Paiute horticulture. During the 1850s irrigated fields as large as ten acres were apparently fairly common (Brooks 1972).

Social Organization

While data regarding subsistence patterns are fairly clear through the archaeological and ethnological records, data regarding precontact Paiute social and political organization are vague and often contradictory.[3] It is generally assumed that kinship was reckoned on a bilateral basis, and both individuals and families appear to have shifted their residence with ease. According to Kelly (1964:25–26, 93–94, 99–100), her informants stated that the Paiutes practiced matrilocal residence, but her data did not indicate that this was indeed the rule.[4] Some informants suggest that they practiced brother-sister avoidance after puberty. Informants also hint at various matrifocal arrangements; by the late 1980s, it seems impossible to make any definitive statements from these vague allusions. The available information is not conclusive enough to develop a detailed anthropological model of their social organization nor to make definitive statements about the character of Paiute band structures in the pre- or protohistoric period.

William Palmer, an amateur historian, has been the most forthright in dealing with this problem:

At the onset it should be said that this study is not exhaustive. The task has been undertaken too late, perhaps, to ever make it so. There are very few Indians living today who can remember with clearness the days when the tribes were living on their own home lands and it has taken a great deal of probing to bring out the information that is given herein. (1933:90)

Our knowledge of the lives of the Paiutes, as well as those of many other Indian groups, is quite limited, even for the years between 1880 and 1970; ethnographers have been more interested in reconstructing the past than in recording the contemporary lives of their informants. As d'Azevedo (1966:103) notes, "In the Great Basin area, at least, there has been until very recently an almost total absence of study of ongoing Indian communities—of reservations, colonies or scattered settlements." Consequently there has been a long-running debate in the literature regarding the nature of Paiute band organization.[5] Scholars who have dealt with this issue seem to agree that their organization was family-based and bilateral and that families cooperated in the formation of larger groups. Kelly (1964:25–26) and C. Fowler (1982a) report that the Paiutes usually lived in independent, acephalous groups of from three to ten households. Powell and Ingalls (1874:3) report that the Basin groups numbered between forty and three hundred people.

C. Fowler (1982a, 1982b) suggests that the camp group was of primary importance for the Paiute. Such a unit was an informally led cluster of from three to ten families who cooperated on a regular basis and usually wintered together. She points out (1982a) that groupings larger than extended families seem to have taken their names from staple foods or major resources. This is true of the Cedar Band, one of whose aboriginal names is "Kumoits," referring to rabbits. Band names may have been based more on resources and geography and less on political orientation than Palmer (1933) postulated. Powell and Ingalls (1874:11) listed eight "tribes" of Utah Paiutes in the early 1870s (see table 2). They named Taugu as the principal chief of the eight Utah

Table 2. *Utah Paiute "Tribes" in the 1870s*

Tribe	Location
1. Kwiumpus	Vicinity of Beaver
2. Paruguns	Vicinity of Parowan
3. UnkapaNukuints	Vicinity of Cedar
4. Paspikaivats	Vicinity of Toquerville
5. Unkakaniguts	Long Valley
6. Paguits	Pagu Lake
7. Kaivavwits	Vicinity of Kanab
8. UaiNuints	Vicinity of St. George

and three northern Arizona tribes. Palmer (1933:96–97) recorded a list of thirty-five Paiute bands (table 3 excludes the Pahvants and the non-Utah bands; also shown is the list of ten Utah bands compiled by Kelly 1934:558–59).

Despite confusion over terminology and criteria, Palmer's list corresponds more closely to Powell's than does Kelly's (Steward 1955a:30–31). My conclusions from reviewing these three lists and the Mormon documents from the 1850s, are that eighteen groups, and undoubtedly others, existed prior to or concurrently with the arrival of the Mormons (see table 4 and figure 1).

Differences in band identification may have been the result of these authors referring to separate levels of social organization. Palmer, for instance, was not a trained ethnographer and may have included names of food-use areas, family groupings, and bands, without rigorously establishing which level of organization was being designated by his informants. Another factor that may account for a lack of consistency in band names is the dramatic changes that were taking place in Paiute life when data were gathered on their social organization. Euler (1966:103), discounting the existence of precontact Paiute bands, concludes that "In sum, Southern Paiute bands were post-contact phenomena that had their roots in the combination of camp groups and the rise of men of prestige."

Stoffle and Dobyns (1982:47–49; Stoffle, Dobyns, and Evans 1983: 7–9) divided the southern Paiutes into western and eastern subdivi-

Table 3. *Paiute Bands according to Palmer and Kelly*

Palmer 1933	Kelly 1934
1. Turoonkwints	San Juan
2. Toyebeits/Toyweapits	Kaiparowits
3. Quiumputs	Panguitch
4. Indian Peak	Kaibab
5. Paraguns	Uinkaret
6. Parupits	Shivwits
7. Assichoots	St. George
8. Kumoits/Wahnkwints	Cedar
9. Taveatsooks	Gunlock
10. Paroosits	Beaver
11. Tonoquints	
12. Matooshats	
13. Paweapits	
14. Iooguneintz	
15. Unkakanigits	
16. Paepas	

sions, with head chiefs. They also speculated that the Southern Paiutes were more tightly organized than any previous authors had indicated. They suggested that the two tribal subdivisions were presided over by a paramount chief and that higher and lesser chiefs were differentiated from the population of followers (see section on leadership, below).

It seems obvious that, as early as 1858, both diseases and the loss of their best land forced the Paiutes into new, composite political structures. Powell and Ingalls (1874:14) stated that groups of tribes were organized into confederacies under a head chief. Where there had originally been several tribes, there was at the time of their writing "only one united tribe." Their reference to the Pahranigats specifically lists white pressure as the reason for the uniting of three separate tribes.

A question beyond the number and location of groups is whether these named groupings constituted true bands. The data available to us are inconsistent in a number of areas: the delineation of named territorial and residence groupings; and the character of the sociopolitical organization of these groupings. Bands are usually defined by coopera-

Table 4. *Paiute Groups at the Time of*
Mormon Colonialization

1. Parowan area
2. Cedar City area: two to seven groups
3. Santa Clara: three to seven groups
4. Harmony
5. Virgin River: multiple groups
6. Panquitch Lake
7. Ash Creek: Two groups?
8. Uinkarets
9. Beaver Dam area
10. Kaiparowits
11. San Juan: two groups
12. Antarianunts.

tion "in a sufficient number of economic and social activities under central control to have acquired a community of interest" (Steward 1938:181). While some extrafamily cooperation existed among the Paiutes, there is little agreement on the extent and structure of this cooperation. Steward (1938, 1955a, 1970), on the one hand, concluded that the Southern Paiutes lacked the natural-resource base to support true band divisions. He (1970:393) noted that "unusual concentration of resources . . . might have provided preconditions favorable to incipient band development." Stewart (1942), in contrast, seems to have taken Southern Paiute band structure as a given for all hunter-gatherers, and Kelly (1934, 1964), with some reservations, attributed band status to the Kaibab Paiute. Part of the discrepancy, according to C. Fowler, may reflect Steward's lack of attention to regional variations in both resources and social organization. C. Fowler (1982b:126) pointed out that Steward drew his data and conclusions from only two Nevada groups and did not consider bands occupying richer riverine environments, such as those of southwestern Utah. Steward's report written for the Paiute Land Claims Case (1955a), however, summarized the historical literature on the riverine Southern Paiute and still concluded that they lacked true bands. The resources available to the Paiute living along the Virgin and Santa Clara rivers were certainly "unusual concentrations" when compared with those of the Nevada Paiute. The Paiutes along the Santa Clara, Virgin, and Muddy rivers seem to have met several criteria that would have provided a material base for social organization beyond the extended family. These include larger population concentrations, horticulture, and access to a fairly dependable and rich faunal and floral resource base.[6]

Exactly how exclusive these territories were and to what extent resources were subject to individual ownership is not clear. Nevertheless sworn affidavits, gathered by William Palmer for the Indian Claims Commission in 1949–50 (Holt 1990), suggest that Shivwit informants clearly recognized definite boundaries for the Cedar band. The nine affidavits, from Shivwits, Parowan, and Cedar band members and one white are remarkably consistent as to band boundaries and strongly suggest that resources within these boundaries were considered band property, so that band members had first rights of use, at the very least. Seasonal forays into land claimed by other groups was, however, common. Diaries from the 1840s and 1850s indicate that the Southern Paiutes then lived in larger groups than did those who survived the 1860s and that they spent a significant amount of time cultivating crops (Hafen and Hafen 1954b; Brooks 1972). Depopulation during the second half of the nineteenth century most certainly led to the consolidation of groups, in order to maintain their viability.

Clearly the Southern Paiute designated themselves by geographic regions and food names, and at least some of these groupings were true bands by Steward's 1938 definition. These camp groups consisted of a series of households linked by kinship, the specialized knowledge of certain part-time specialists, and other ties, such as marriage and friendship. These multifamily units were held together by the limited authority of leaders and by recognized, but highly flexible, membership rules. Most contemporary informants claim that territories were well known and that permission was always sought when one group wanted to utilize resources within the territory of another group. With the arrival of the Mormon settlers, the various Paiute groups coalesced, in an attempt to survive in their changed environment.

Leadership

Many older contemporary informants seem to have rather clear notions of the functions and power of the Paiute "chiefs," or leaders, who are referred to as *neab* or *niavi* (Holt fieldnotes 1982). It may be said that leadership for the Southern Paiutes was complex and subtle. Authority flows from group consensus, and leaders can only be effective to the extent that their actions and opinions reflect that of the group consensus (see chapter 6 for the contemporary situation). One primary function, at least in the period from 1900 to 1930, was to rise early and exhort the group to begin their subsistence chores: "he would tell them (when) he wanted them to do anything . . . Go you guys—go hunting—we're going to eat meat—we're going to eat it or starve" (Holt fieldnotes 1982). Their other prime function was to determine and then act as a spokesman for the group's consensus. The *niav* seems to have enjoyed limited authority based on consent (most often task-specific authority) and limited personal power based on special abilities in such activities as healing, hunting, mediating, and creating consensus. Some informants suggest that "you had to do what he said" when it came to subsistence activities and that the *niav* was also the person approached by Paiutes from other areas for permission to hunt and gather within the territory of his group.

White settlers assumed that the Paiute "chiefs" had more authority than they actually did. As early as 1855, Mormon settlers were "setting apart" as chiefs those Paiutes who were allied with them (*Deseret News* 1855). The Mormon practice of appointing band leaders and backing those Paiutes who stressed accommodation with whites may have led to factional splits within Paiute groups. The Paiute concept of limited, situational leadership has survived, despite over 135 years of efforts by both the Mormon church and the federal government to replace it with the Anglo image of leadership (Braithwaite 1972; Holt 1987). As we shall see in later chapters, tribal council members are still hesitant to take charge of situations or to appear too authoritarian.

The Paiutes' lack of military power and their limited corporate organization made it difficult to either assimilate or to annihilate them. As were lowland tribes in South America, Paiutes were utilized as household servants and agricultural laborers (Service 1955). Once they were deprived of other options, however, they were particularly vulnerable to the leadership of white colonists. In general the Paiutes' active response to this process was one of accommodation to the paternalistic tendencies of Mormon (and later BIA) authority figures. They adapted by ostensibly going along with the imposed policies of assimilation, dependency, and religious conversion, while, at the same time, they remained hostile to many aspects of white culture and attempted to preserve the family-based core of their aboriginal culture.

The *niavi* were integrated into the Mormon system, and the Paiute leaders became the administrators of policies made by whites. In 1855 the Mormon missionary Jacob Hamlin wrote, "So far we have managed to gain much influence amongst them. As for myself, I have sought the Lord much for understanding. I have always found something or some way to govern and control them" (Hamlin 1854–57:18). At this point their ability to initiate directions and policies, independent of white oversight, declined, and they began to react to white suggestions and initiatives. The Mormons aided in the selection of Paiute leaders into the early twentieth century (E. H. Anderson 1900:515). This suggests that even some of our earliest information on leaders and their following had already been affected by changes and a growing Anglo presence; all efforts to discover the character of precontact Paiute sociopolitical organization must take these early transformations into account.

> Chieftainship seems to have been the result of the amalgamation of camp groups due to Anglo encroachments on Paiute lands and the rise, in these consolidations, of men of some prestige who could represent the Indians before the Anglos, as well as to lead defensive and minor offensive military operations. It should not be overlooked, however, that these chiefs might have been declared such by the Anglos solely because of cooperation. (Euler 1966:102)

A contrary interpretation has been advanced by Stoffle and Dobyns (1982), suggesting that a Paiute principal chief had a greater role prior to white contact. They maintained that there existed "an aboriginal elite composed of theocratic chiefs . . ." (1982:47). They stated that this priestly elite was marked by a special language and that its members were the only ones allowed to wear turquoise. This "highly speculative" interpretation seems to be based on the Chemehuevi work of Laird (1976:24), some ethnohistorical inferences, and, perhaps, undocumented information from their informants. They found three hierarchical levels in Paiute society: high chiefs, lesser chiefs, and followers. They also mentioned a specialized class of runners (1982:48) that carried "messages from theocratic leaders to local social units." Stoffle and Dobyns may be correct about the use of runners; I have seen several fragmentary references to the use of runners by the Cedar City Paiute leader. They claim that the existence of these runners negates Steward's and others' descriptions of Southern Paiute society as atomistic. Without any evidence to the contrary, however, one must assume that they relied heavily on Laird's Chemehuevi material. The Chemehuevis, while linguistically very similar to the Southern Paiutes, have been culturally influenced by the Yuman peoples. Data from the Chemehuevis can therefore not be indiscriminately applied to the Southern Paiutes.

After reviewing the early accounts of Mormon missionaries (Hamlin 1854–57, Brooks 1972) and travelers, I am convinced that characteristic differences existed among Paiute groups, to the extent that they were perceived as two separate groups by early observers: those with a riverine orientation and those with a nonriverine orientation. The early accounts generally refer to the riverine groups as Pahutes and to the nonriverine groups as Piedes (Hamlin 1859; Simpson 1869:44–45). Thomas Brown's diary is very explicit about the differences he noticed:

> On returning we saw four Indians coming down a mountain from the east with 2 horses . . . They are one days journey from their wickeups, are taller and appear more intellectual. They call themselves Pahutes and are taller than the Parides, I believe them to be of the same tribe, but pronounce the name differently. They are handsomer and more intelligent. (Brooks 1972:49)

The riverine groups depended more on horticulture, whereas the nonriverine groups depended primarily on foraging.[7] Consequently the riverine groups probably had a nutritional advantage. Whatever differences existed aboriginally between "Pahute" and "Pahede," they were wiped out in the 1860s, as the Mormons poured into their territory and survivors began to merge into composite bands for survival. Despite the tenuous nature of the evidence, it seems probable that: there were two limited clusters of bands, one based on the Muddy and another based on the Santa Clara; Paiute bands did exist in the presence of riverine environments and horticulture; nonriverine Paiutes probably operated only in terms of extended families, yet were tied through kinship with the riverine groups, to the extent that membership in either group might shift with relative ease; thus Paiute society, although it was flexible and loose, was not atomistic, but possessed structure, boundaries, and cooperative action.

Myth and Ritual

As is true of many other aspects of their culture, the precontact cosmology of the Paiutes is not well understood.[8] Their oral tradition is very rich and includes myths and tales as well as songs and proverbial aphorisms. Winter was a period of low mobility, and Paiute groups appear to have remained within ten to fifteen kilometers of their winter camps (C. Fowler 1982b:127). Tales and myths were to be told only in the winter, "because the snakes will bite you if you tell them" at another time (Holt fieldnotes, 1982). Traditional Paiutes believed that all things, including inanimate objects, were alive. Sometimes an animal was just an animal; at other times, it was a spirit animal—it had powers, and could influence the human situation (Palmer 1936b, 1942).

Like many other Native Americans, the traditional Paiutes believed in twin creator gods: Tabuts (Tauwats, Tipaci) was the elder brother and was symbolized by the wolf; Shinawav (*Shinau-wau, Shenobe, Sinawapi*) was the younger brother, who sometimes appeared in the guise of a coyote. These two brothers lived in a cave in Mt. Charleston, in southern Nevada. Tabuts attempted to order a perfect world; Shinawav sometimes acted as the messenger of Tabuts and intermediary with the Paiutes. However he was also often the mischievous trickster coyote, sometimes hero and sometimes seducer of women. Many Paiute myths involve Shinawav reversing the work of Tabuts.

The Paiute theory of disease suggests that sickness is caused by intrusive evil spirits, soul-loss, or the work of an evil shaman. According to Kelly (1939:154), "To the Shivwits disease is caused by intrusion, either of an object or of a ghost; and perhaps occasionally by soul loss." Sapir (1910) notes that the Southern Paiute medicine man (*puagant*) may either be male or female, and "the power of doctoring is not acquired by a period of fasting or training in the mountains, but may be acquired in the ordinary course of life (after puberty and before 30–40 years of age) by dreaming." Contemporary informants suggest that power was acquired by prayer, fasting, and dreaming. A shaman was often identified by his mustache (Beckwith 1975:27) or his cane (Kelly 1939:158). Palmer (1936, 1956) agrees with this interpretation, but found two different types of shamans or, at least, two distinct styles of curing: "The doctor is a faith healer while the medicine man drives the demons of disease away with concoctions of dried lizard blood, burnt crow feathers, or whatever else his spirit tutor advises him to use" (1936b:535).

Informants who were in their late sixties and early seventies during the years 1982–84 confirmed the two approaches. One stated that "[Jake Wiggits] was a doctor, not a medicine man—he would sing on them—sing on them, lay down on them and suck it out of them" (Holt fieldnotes 1982). Kelly (1939) reinforces this interpretation by noting two types of shaman: the dreamer and the regular shaman. Brown (Brooks 1972:23) gave an interesting, first-hand account of a Paiute shaman's sucking cure, which also included hot water, singing, pressure, and expectorating "dark green stones—about the size of a bean."

Traditionally the Utah Paiute had a very rich store of songs. Their most traditional dance was the circle, or round, dance, and round-dance songs are the most numerous of the Paiute songs. Other Paiute songs include the scalp dance, gambling songs, and songs for supernatural power. The bear dance and turkey dance were borrowed from the Utes (Sapir 1910, Stewart 1942:349). Kelly and Fowler (1987:384) mentioned other dances, one dealing with prophecy and another acquired from the Western Shoshones. Traditional dances appear to have ceased at Cedar City and Shivwits around 1950 and at Richfield in the early 1960s; however, I was told that in 1988 the Kaibab Paiutes held a bear dance in April, and the Richfield group has also attempted to revive the bear dance.

When a young boy killed his first deer, he distributed the meat around the camp and kept none of it for himself. This custom is still being practiced at Kanosh. Often boys were told to take a cold bath and wash away their childhood. Older unmarried women often initiated young men into the mysteries of sex. Some of the young men lived for a while with these older women, and at other times they merely slept together, with the young men leaving the older women gifts.

At menarche girls were separated from the group and were given instruction in the duties of women and the value of hard work. During this period of separation they were not allowed to touch their hair, to scratch without using a scratching stick, or to eat meat. During their periods women were considered dangerous; contact with menstrual blood was said to lessen the power of males and make them lazy.

Girls were considered women and marriageable after menarche. Boys could marry when they were considered to be reliable hunters. By the historic period, a man who wanted to marry a particular woman would announce his intentions and offer to wrestle for her. Brown (Brooks 1972:149–51) describes a two-day brawl over a woman. This may have been the result of the reduced number of women available because of the slave trade (see below). Many marriages were apparently arranged by the parents. There were no special rites of marriage; the couple would simply begin living together. While most marriages were monogamous, there were instances of polygyny (a man marrying two sisters) and, less frequently, of polyandry.

Pregnant women were told to use a scratching stick and were to drink warm water before and after the birth of a child. Birth usually took place away from the main camp, in a brush shelter. Babies were delivered with the mother standing. After the birth the mother and her child were placed on a bed heated by rocks placed in a fire. Mothers were not supposed to eat meat for a month after the birth.

Men with pregnant wives were also told to use a scratching stick and to eat no meat for a week after the birth. They were not allowed to sleep the night after the birth and the next day had to take a cold bath.

The mourning ceremony (*yaxap*, "cry" or "sing") is the Paiutes' funeral rite, generally known today as the memorial sing. This ritual is thought to have its origins with the Mohave and to have reached the Paiutes toward the end of the nineteenth century (Sapir 1930–31, Kelly 1964:95). While ancestors were respected, their ghosts were feared traditionally. They still avoid to some extent the dead person's name in general conversation, and they also avoid the word "dead." The conventional usage today is to say: "she has passed away," or "he is gone now."

While the major purpose of the cry is to respect and remember the dead, most informants also state that property was destroyed, in order to send it along with the departed. According to Sapir's fieldnotes (1910), "The object of "cry" is to show respect for dead relatives; no idea of sending property to spirit world, but goods are sacrificed merely to show love and disregard of wealth for their sake."

Palmer (1936a) attended a cry held in August of 1935; he quoted a cry leader as saying:

We have cried for all the dead that we cannot remember. Now we will cry for the ones that we have known. We will cry for those whose names we want remembered as long as we live. Some have died since last year and all the tribe has never cried for them yet. We will cry for them first. Their families will call their names.

As of 1990 there may be as many as one hundred songs in the Utah Paiute repertoire sometimes associated with the cry. Although the most ubiquitous song is the salt song, mountain sheep songs, bird songs, and coyote songs are also part of the cry repertoire. Today only a handful (ten to fifteen?) of the older Paiutes are able to put on a mourning ceremony.[9] This group serves all the Utah Paiutes and occasionally other groups in Arizona and Nevada. Today (1990) there are two types of sings: the first is held on the death of a particular individual; the second is held one year after the death of an individual or on Memorial Day, to remember all the dead. Traditionally the cry lasted three or four days; often on the last night, property, usually belonging to the deceased individual, was burned or destroyed.

In 1990 the typical sing at Cedar City occurs on the night before interment. Cry songs are sung in a certain ritual order. The family of the deceased person displays important personal effects of the deceased, some of which are interred with the body, others of which are destroyed. The host family is responsible for feeding the mourners and for providing cigarettes and coffee. The women cry and openly display their grief, while the men are more reserved. On the following morning, a service is usually held, at the Mormon Indian Branch chapel. At this service family, friends, and usually the local Mormon bishop speak. The burial then takes place in the Paiute section of the Cedar City cemetery. Funerals create a strong obligation among the Paiutes to attend; not a few people have lost their jobs because they missed work to attend a funeral.

European Contacts

It is difficult to overestimate the impact on Paiute life of the swift occupation of their lands by Mormon colonists. The Southern Paiutes' culture and the physical environment to which they were adapted were furiously assaulted by the white interlopers. Every aspect of their subsistence system and social organization were affected by traders, immigrants, and government officials. By understanding the magnitude of this white impact one can also better grasp those facets of Paiute culture that have acted to protect their way of life from total assimilation.

After the Domínguez-Escalante expedition of 1776, other Spanish traders followed; by the 1813 expedition of Arze and García, it was reported that there had already been a slave trade in Utah for several years (Malouf and Malouf 1945:378–396). Utah remained, however, on the periphery of Spanish activity in North America and was never settled. In the early nineteenth century, Paiutes were a major source of slaves for the Utes and New Mexicans. Although Spain outlawed slave trading in 1812, Snow (1929:69) concluded that "almost continuously from Escalante's expedition on until after the Mormons came, wandering Spaniards entered these Valleys [Salt Lake, Utah, and Sevier], not only for furs, but to traffic in Indian slaves." The extent to which this slaving and the introduction of European diseases disrupted the Paiutes' lifestyle is undocumented, but there are hints that the popu-

lation was reduced considerably. There is little doubt that slaving created an imbalance in the sex ratio, since young girls were a primary
object of the slavers. This is substantiated by Indian Agent Garland
Hurt, who reported that prior to 1860, the slave trade had reduced
the Paiute population to the point where, "scarcely one-half of the Py-
eed children are permitted to grow up in a band" (Malouf and Malouf
1945:384). The 1874 report of Powell and Ingalls listed the following
population figures:

	Utes	Paiutes
MEN	174	233
WOMEN	167	148
CHILDREN	215	97

While the accuracy of these figures is doubtful, the ratios of men to
women and of women to children is dramatic. For the Utes the ratio
of men to women was 1:0.96; for the Paiutes it was 1:0.64. For the
Utes the ratio of women to children was 1:1.29, for the Paiutes it was
1:0.65. Jacob Hamlin (1854–57:10) relates that the Southern Paiutes
fought over women because there were "from six to twenty wanting
her for a wife." Another hypothesis is that the effects of the slave trade
have been overestimated whereas the effects of the Mormon invasion
and its associated diseases have been underestimated. Brown's journal (Brooks 1972:60–61) noted that on the Santa Clara, the riverine
Paiute women had "two or three children apiece," and at the camp
there were "six squaws and ten children."

The slave trade affected not only the population size and sex ratio of
the Paiutes but also their land-use strategies, by forcing them to move
into more-protected areas, thus lowering their foraging and horticultural production. Brown's journal (Brooks 1972), for one, mentioned
Paiute camps in inaccessible spots. Their strategy was to move and/or
hide, to avoid violence or overwhelming force. Slaving must have also
affected the quantity and types of food available, since the Southern
Paiutes practiced a sexual division of labor, in which females gathered
wild resources, providing a significant portion of the calories consumed
by the family groups.

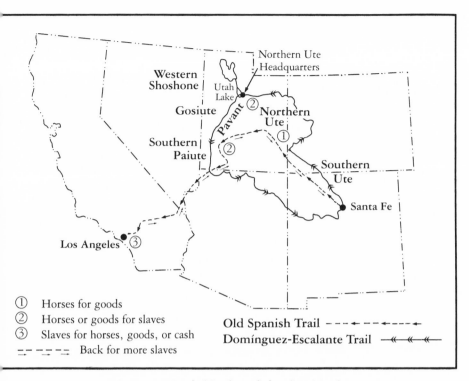

Figure 2. *Early Trails and the Slave Trade*

The other major early contact with the Paiutes was the commercial traffic opened through their territory by the Yount-Wolfskill party, in 1830 (Alley 1982:118). The Old Spanish Trail passed through the core of the Paiute homeland and was utilized by both slavers and other traders (see figure 2). The Trail gave the slavers direct access to their Paiute victims (Alley 1982:118), and led to an influx of domesticated livestock into Paiute country. The Southern Paiutes were soon faced not only with the Utes stealing their children for the slave trade, but also with the prospect of thousands of horses and cattle eating the plants that they utilized for food. Traffic through the Paiute lands increased in 1848, as immigrants flocked to California and the gold rush began. These intrusions necessarily contributed further to the decline of the Paiute resource base.

Of this time Euler writes that:

Acculturation, therefore was much more rapid for Paiutes living along rivers such as the Muddy, the Virgin, and the Santa Clara and the smaller creeks like Beaver, Coal and Ash. In spite of numerous contacts on the trails, however, change and stress had but begun for the Paiute. (1966:54)

The slave trade and the environmental damage done by travelers dramatically foreshadowed the carnage that was to come with white settlement; these early contacts eroded the Paiutes' ability to withstand the later pressures on their economy and culture. They were extremely vulnerable and powerless in any direct confrontation with well-armed, mounted intruders. While it is clear that these forces drastically changed the lives of the Paiutes and diminished both their ability and their will to resist colonization, the early interlopers did not stay to settle in Paiute territory. Thus although Paiute sovereignty was disrupted by slavery and the commercial traffic through their homeland, their rights to their land, social organization, and culture remained intact until the coming of the Mormon colonists.

Mormon Ideology and the Indian

Mormon theology confers special meaning to the American Indian (Vogel 1986). They are believed to be descendants of Jewish tribes who migrated by boat to the western hemisphere in a series of migrations between the time of the Tower of Babel and around 600 B.C. To the outsider the Mormon doctrine concerning Indians, or Lamanites, as they are called, is surprisingly dualistic, since the Indians are seen at the same time as both a cursed and a chosen people. In the Mormon church's major scripture, the *Book of Mormon*, the prophet Mormon characterizes this accursed nature: "This people shall be scattered, and shall become a dark, a filthy, and a loathsome people, beyond the description of that which ever hath been amongst us, yea, even that which hath been among the Lamanites, and this because of their unbelief and idolatry" (Mormon 5:15).

The last days, however, hold the promise of special status for Indians. The *Book of Mormon* states that "their scales of darkness shall begin to fall from their eyes; and many generations shall not pass away among them, save they shall be a white and delightsome people" (2 Nephi 30:6). Speaking in 1957 Spencer W. Kimball, who was to become the Mormon president, said:

> We [the LDS church] have a definite responsibility to the Lamanites [Indians]. . . . It is my conviction that the end will not come; that the closing scene will not be ushered in; that the Lord himself will not come in His Glory until a substantial part of the Lamanites have had the gospel preached to them. . . . We are in the last days. Time is short. (E. Wilkinson and Arrington 1976:505–6)

The salvation of the Indian plays an important part in Mormon eschatology: "helping" the Indian also helps to further the ultimate goals of the Mormon church.[10]

Because of the Paiute diet and subsistence activities, early travelers often characterized them as "diggers." The Mormon image of the Paiute Indian also fits the digger stereotype quite accurately; that is, low intellect, laziness, uncleanliness, and ignobleness (Lonnberg 1981:215–20). This attitude is reflected in the words of Hosea Stout, an early Mormon diarist: "The Indians of the Rio Virgin and Muddy are the most low and contemptible I ever saw and show the most degraded and dishonest disposition" (Brooks 1964 2:461).

The Mormon missionary Jacob Hamlin, who spent much of his life working with Indians, echoed those sentiments:

> They are in a very low, degraded condition indeed; loathsome & filthy beyond description. I have wished many times for the moment, that my lot was cast among a more cleanly people; where there could be found something desirable, something cheering to a person accustomed to a civilized life. (Hamlin 1854–57: 17–18)

There was little new in the Mormon image of the Indians as degraded and under the control of Satan, as this belief can be traced all the way back to the works of Richard Hakluyt of 1582 and 1600 (Cave 1985). Conversely the belief that the natives were chosen led to their comparatively mild treatment, by frontier standards, and to their official treatment as wayward children to be slowly civilized and assimilated. Thomas O'Dea (1957:256) remarked upon this bifurcated view of the Indian by suggesting that the Mormons held both missionary and colonist views. The theological, or missionary, view stressed the Indian as convert and chosen, while the pioneer view stressed his savage, fallen nature.

This dual ideology led to a Mormon policy of paternalism, based on a claim of uplifting the fallen Indian. The Mormons often made metaphorical use of the word "child" in explaining their relationship toward the Paiutes. This desire to "help the Indians" resulted in a pattern by which the Mormons initiated every major step in the lives of the Paiutes until the restoration of tribal status, in 1980.

Although Mormon ideology traditionally stresses self-help, the Paiutes were seen as being incapable of making even the simplest decision. They had lost control of their environment, and what initiative the Paiutes did take was channeled into approved activities by local church leaders. The power asymmetry between colonists and Paiutes was legitimized by the parent-child metaphor. As the Mormon historian Juanita Brooks has stated (1944:1), "The Mormon philosophy regarding the Indians is unique; the Mormon treatment of their dark-skinned neighbors was determined largely by that ideology." Perhaps it would be more accurate to say that the manner in which the Mormons assumed and ensured their dominance over the Paiutes and other Great Basin Indians was a unique combination of conquest and paternalism.

Settlement and Submission

With the arrival of Mormon colonists in southern Utah, in 1851, a period of accelerated change began for the Paiutes. The Mormons envisioned their own theocratic state as combining both secular and sacred functions. During the nineteenth century, there was little separation of church and state, and virtually all personal and public activities were influenced or controlled by the Mormon church. As Evans (1938:94) explained, "All things merged in the church. It was the legislative, judicial, and executive body operating through its delegated ministry. It embraced all things, secular and civil. . . . The bishop and his counselors were the deliberate body that justified matters of policy." In creating their Zion, the Mormons attempted to plant colonies along a corridor from Salt Lake City to San Bernardino, California, in order to establish a sea route to Utah and to promote economic independence from the United States.

It took the Mormons only fifteen years to found colonies at most of the best agricultural sites in Paiute country. Settlements were established at Parowan and Cedar City in 1851, at Las Vegas in 1857, St. George in 1861, and along the Moapa River in 1865.

The Paiutes welcomed the first Mormons and provided them with food; they viewed the Mormons as a means of protection from the slave raids of the Utes and Mexicans. Alley (1982:123) explained their warm welcome of the Mormons in this manner: "The settlers offered a buffer for the Southern Paiutes, a barrier to their many enemies. Moreover, they offered access to the technology and knowledge neighbors had so long used to the Paiutes' disadvantage."

The Southern Paiutes practiced a lifestyle that was based on kinship and reciprocity, and their adaptation to the Anglo-Mormon invaders mirrored their understanding of such a system. Faced with overwhelming power, they adapted by "giving up" their land, in exchange for the promise that the Mormons would look after them and their children. In the Paiute view, gifts from the whites flow from this "treaty"; thus reciprocity and dependence are intertwined.

Contrary to the expectations of the Paiutes, however, the Mormons, at least through 1851, appeared to encourage the slave raids of Ute leaders such as Wakara. The leader of the Mormon colony in southern Utah, George A. Smith, even provided Wakara with a letter of introduction, which stated that "they wished to trade horses, Buckskins and Piede children we hope them success and Prosperity and good bargains" (Inter-tribal Council 1976:61).

The slave trade was outlawed in 1852, and the territorial legislature, while complaining that the Indian title to the soil had not been extinguished, passed an act entitled "For the Relief of Indian Slaves and Prisoners." This act established Indian "indentures," which could not exceed twenty years. The master was supposed "to send said apprentice to school, if there be a school in the district or vicinity for the term of three months in each year, at a time when said Indian child shall be between the ages of seven and sixteen" (Brooks 1944:8–9). Anyone possessing any "Indian prisoner, child or woman" was to appear before a selectman or probate judge, and it would then be determined if the person was suitable and qualified to "raise, or retain and educate said Indian prisoner" (Snow 1929:84–86).

By the mid-1850s the Paiutes were experiencing a severe food shortage; they sold their children to the Mormons rather than watch them starve. During his first visit to what would become Parowan, Brigham Young said that he:

> Advised them to buy up the Lamanite children as fast as they could, educate them and teach them the gospel, so that many generations would not pass ere they should become a white and delightsome people. . . . I knew the Indians would dwindle away, but let a remnant of the seed of Joseph be saved. (Brooks 1944:6)

If they sold to the local Mormons, at least the Paiute parents would know where their children were. Nevertheless the vast majority of the children acquired by Mormons died from disease. Thomas Brown (Brooks 1972) noted that three of five children he had acquired died within a one-year period. In Young's 1852 gubernatorial address to the Utah legislature, he was quick to draw a distinction between Mexican slavery and Mormon servitude:

> Under the present low and degraded situation of the Indian race, so long as the practice of gambling away, selling, and otherwise disposing of their children; as also sacrificing prisoners obtains among them, it seems indeed that any transfer would be to them a relief and a benefit.
>
>   . . . This may be said to present a new feature in the traffic of human beings; it is essentially purchasing them into freedom instead of slavery; but it is not the low, servile drudgery of Mexican slavery, to which I would doom them, not to be raised among beings scarcely superior to themselves, but where they could find that consideration pertaining not only to civilized, but humane and benevolent society. (Brooks 1944:7)

From the early beginnings of the Mormon settlement of their country, Paiute labor played an important role in the economy of southern Utah. Mormon towns were established on the west side of the mountains where streams descended; these very locations were core areas for various Paiute bands. The economy of these bands, in the immediate path of Mormon settlement, almost instantly shifted to fill the labor needs of the settlers. The original justification for colonies in Paiute country was the iron deposits discovered near the future site of Cedar City. As the settlers claimed the prime lands that the Paiutes had previously foraged upon, the Southern Paiutes were quickly forced to become a source of cheap labor for the settlers. Like so many other Indians in the West, "they were forced by economic circumstances to become agricultural laborers or house servants for white people" (Forbes 1974:61). They gathered near the settlements and began to work for a meal, piece of clothing, or some manufactured article.

In one of the few recorded sympathetic views of the Paiutes, William Adams, writing from the settlement at Parowan, stated that:

I will say this much concerning the Indians—only for their labor, there would have been hundreds of bushels of produce lost, that could not have been saved by the white population. I consider myself a common hand, to work, but I must give up to some of the Piedes for quickness, and the Pahvantes (Indians) work considerable, but not so willingly as the Piedes or Pahutes. We have had from 20 to 40 lodges here through the summer and fall, averaging from one to two hundred natives. (Adams 1852)

Mormon Indian Policy

As early as 1850, Brigham Young asked John M. Berhisel, a Mormon lobbyist in Washington, to persuade government officials to "extinguish" Indian title to the Great Basin and thus legalize Mormon settlement and land claims (Coates 1969:175).

Dibble (1947:65–66) explained that Mormon Indian policy, as expressed by Brigham Young, was threefold in purpose: "first, to bring the Indians forcibly to terms; second, to teach them the white man's ethics, preferably by example; and third, to bring them into the religious fold." In May of 1853, Young said that "when we first entered Utah, we were prepared to meet all the Indians in these mountains, and kill every soul of them if we had been obliged so to do" (Dibble 1947:66).

Exterminating the Indians was costly in terms of lives, property and, in the Mormon case, doctrinal cohesiveness. In a message to the Utah territorial legislature (*Deseret News* 1854), Young articulated the second phase of his policy: "I have uniformly pursued a friendly course towards them, feeling convinced that independent of the question of exercising humanity toward so degraded and ignorant a race of people, it was manifestly more economical and less expensive to feed and clothe them than to fight them."

In October of 1853, Brigham Young established the Southern Indian Mission, whose assignment it was:

> . . . not to help white men, but to save the red ones, learn their language, and you can do this more effectually by living among them as well as writing down a list of words, go with them where they go, live with them and when they rest let them live with you, feed them, clothe them and teach them as you can, and being thus with you all the time, you will soon be able to teach them in their own language, they are our brethren, we must seek after them, commit their language, get to their understanding, and when they go off in parties you go with them. (Brooks 1972:30)

Young's stress on learning the native language and on close association with the Indians appears to have been similar to that of the Jesuits (Axtell 1981:69–70). Mormon missionaries were assigned to the Paiutes and arrived in Harmony in 1854. For several years their efforts to convert the Paiutes remained relatively strenuous; but by 1858, Jacob Hamlin acknowledged that the mission to the Paiute had not been successful and that such efforts should be redirected to the Hopi and the Navajo (Hamlin 1854–57:11).

The original design of Mormon leaders had, of course, been to establish an independent, theocratic state. This was thwarted first by the United States victory over Mexico, by which the Mexican territory that the Mormons had occupied became part of the United States, and then by the dispatch of federal troops, in 1857, to ensure the loyalty of the Mormons, which resulted in the so-called Mormon War. During this period Mormons made efforts to ensure the neutrality and perhaps the active participation of the Indians against U.S. forces (Furniss 1960). The hostility generated against the Americans flared up in the fall of 1857, when a wagon train was attacked by a mixed force of Paiutes and Mormon militia, at Mountain Meadows. The Mormons persuaded the immigrants to surrender and then proceeded to kill everyone except children under ten (Brooks 1962:69–109). Attempts, in the style of a tragic "Boston Tea Party," were made to blame the massacre on the Paiutes, but finally, in 1875, John D. Lee, who had been a missionary to the Paiutes, was executed for the killings. What records exist tend to confirm the view that he was merely a scapegoat for a wider and more collective guilt (Brooks 1970:195–210).

Settlement and Dependence

During the 1860s Mormon settlers poured into Paiute territory, as they were assigned to what came to be called the Cotton Mission; much of what remained of the best Paiute campsites, fields, and water sources were appropriated by the Europeans. Paiute agriculture thus declined rapidly in the 1860s. It may be significant that I found no mention of independent Paiute irrigation in Utah between 1870 and the establishment of the reservations.

The Mormon settlers, organized and backed by the church hierarchy in Salt Lake City, had in the few years between 1852 and 1869, imposed their form of ecclesiastical settler capitalism on southern Utah. The Paiutes soon found themselves dispossessed of their land base and the ability to provide themselves with food, shelter, and clothing. A prime example of the loss of valuable land was that of Fish Lake, the home of two groups of Indians who probably became the Koosharem group. Fishing rights in Fish Lake were "sold" to the Fremont Irrigation Company for nine horses, five hundred pounds of flour, one beef steer, and one suit of clothes (Artickels of Agreement 1889). Actually paying the Indians for their land proved to be the exception, since the

Anglo-Mormons usually began to utilize any resources not claimed by other whites without regard for Indian rights. According to William Palmer, a Mormon amateur historian:

If one made a map of the Indian tribal homelands one would find in most cases that their locations were almost identical with the places selected by the Mormon pioneers for settlements. The only reason that our encroachments did not precipitate inter-tribal strife was that we came so rapidly that the problem overwhelmed the natives. (1933:90)

As the flow of Mormon settlers increased, the need for Paiute labor decreased. Raids by the Navajos in the early 1860s were defeated by the scouting of the Paiutes and the efforts of the Mormon militia. This was the last major need of the colonists served by the Paiutes. The natives were quickly forgotten, as the Mormons acquired complete military control over what was once the Paiute homeland.

Under such pressures the Paiute population rapidly declined. Kelly (1939:160) recorded an epidemic "characterized by diarrhea and passage of blood" at Muddy Valley, about 1860, which was so serious that the bodies were not buried in the usual manner but were "dumped into a near-by gully." Angus Woodbury (1944:122) stated that: "Fatalities from disease and the diminution of food supplies were undoubtedly heavy factors in the drastic reduction of the Indian population. Of the estimated thousand Parrusits living along the Virgin River in the 50s and 60s, there was only one survivor."

Thus by 1869 the Paiutes were faced with two options: either to leave their traditional areas and move into the most marginal desert. or plateau "regions of refuge," or to settle at the fringes of the Mormon settlements, to beg and do occasional wage labor. The surviving remnants, pushed from their traditional spring or winter campsites, formed composite groups in ghettos called the "Indian village." The Paiute inhabitants of these villages provided the agricultural economy of southern Utah with a continual supply of cheap seasonal labor.

Having acquired complete control over what was once the Paiute homeland, the Mormons still took care of what remained of "their Indians," but in a paternalistic manner. For instance in 1879, Robert

Gardner, bishop of the Price Ward, wrote to a local Indian leader, saying that they would plow ten acres for the Indians to farm; he finished the letter by saying, "Now, Moqueak, what I say, I mean, and you need not trouble me any more, for more land. I know better what is good for you, than you do yourself" (Brooks 1944:26).

Similarly during the 1880s the St. George Stake appropriated four hundred dollars a year for Indian provisions, clothing, and blankets (Brooks 1944:27). Rarely did the Mormons see beyond their own paternalistic stereotypes and realize that by killing the game and taking the land they were responsible for the pathetic condition of the natives.

2 FROM NEGLECT
to
LETHARGY
The Trust Betrayed

UNITED STATES INDIAN policy has often been viewed as oscillating between two polar opposites: assimilation and segregation (Prucha 1986:64). Both the removal of tribal populations from their traditional lands and segregation on reservations, however, can also be seen, as they have even by their authors, as paternalistic strategies to save the Indians from extermination and to allow time for their assimilation to white civilization, education, and Christianity (Gibson 1980, Cave 1985:9–12). Of course one unstated goal of many in government was always the occupation and exploitation of Indian lands.

The first official governmental contact with the Southern Paiutes came in 1856–57, in the person of Agent George W. Armstrong. Armstrong remarked on the extensive Paiute irrigation and farming projects, that "they depend in a great measure on their little farms or patches for subsistence, there being no game of consequence, and but few fish" (Inter-tribal Council (1976:78). He recommended that the government establish two farmsites for the Paiutes, totalling twelve hundred acres. However, nothing came of this recommendation.

The founding of St. George in 1861, on a Paiute campsite, was indicative of the displacement of the Utah Paiutes during the early 1860s; the influx of Mormons and silver miners set the stage for hostilities. Several skirmishes occurred as the Paiutes resorted to cattle raiding and theft to feed their children.

Then in 1865 a series of treaties was made with the Indians of Utah, in order to end their claims to the land and to remove them to a reservation in the Uintah Basin. Paiute "chiefs, headmen, and delegates" met with the Utah superintendent for Indian affairs, O. H. Irish, at Pinto in northern Washington County and signed a treaty that was an extension of the treaty signed by the Utes earlier at Spanish Fork (Irish 1865). It called for the Paiutes to give up all lands they claimed in Utah and to move to the Uintah Reservation. The head chief at the time was presumably Tutzegubet, a Mormon Indian who would later lose his position and travel to Arizona, to preach Mormonism to other Indians. He was to receive: "one dwelling house and to plough and fence for him five acres of land, and to pay him one hundred ($100.00) per annum for the term of twenty years" (Irish 1865). Upon arrival at the reservation, he would receive oxen and farming implements. Neither Tutzegubet nor the other signers of the treaty represented the Paiutes (the Meadow Valley and Virgin River bands) that had been contesting the white encroachment.

The U.S. Senate failed to ratify this treaty, and the Paiutes were later to find themselves without a treaty to protect their rights. They also refused to leave their homeland, because as Agent Thomas Sale wrote from Meadow Valley, in 1865:

> I have endeavored to induce them to leave their present country and go to the Uintah valley and live on that reservation, but they do not consent. They say they are afraid of the Utahs. It is here proper to remark that the Utah have long been in the habit of stealing the women and children of these Indians and either selling them to the Spaniards or to other tribes; sometimes they were kept as servants. This practice is still continued, and hence their fear of the Utahs, and consequent refusal to settle with them at Uintah. They are willing to get together at some place in their own country, but I think it impossible to get their consent to place them with the Utahs. (Sale 1865:155)

Between 1865 and 1868, a small number of Paiutes joined with Blackhawk's Utes in a series of cattle raids that became known as the Blackhawk War. Most incidents involving Paiutes during this period occurred in southern Utah and Nevada and had nothing to do with the fact that Blackhawk was at war. For the Paiutes the most disastrous incident of the Blackhawk War was the Circleville Massacre, in which at least sixteen Paiutes were killed after they surrendered to Mormon militia. The men were shot while trying to escape and the women and older children's throats were cut as they were brought up from a cellar, one by one (Winkler 1987:18–19).

By the end of the 1860s, the Paiutes were destitute and hungry. Whites were pouring into their land, and they could do nothing to stop them.

Reporting from St. George, in October 1871, Special Agent Charles Powell stated that the Paiutes living in southeastern Nevada and southwestern Utah: "have been neglected at this agency, and most shamefully neglected by their former agent {Captain Fenton, U.S. Army} . . . having never received any clothing or subsistence, save in promises, always broken . . ." (Powell 1871).

Powell suggested that a reservation be established on the Muddy River, at St. Thomas; two years later a reservation was established in Nevada on the Muddy, but few of the Utah Paiutes settled there. Attempts to remove the Paiutes from their homeland were a complete failure.

In 1873 John Wesley Powell and G.W. Engalls headed a special commission for the examination of the Paiutes and other tribes in the Great Basin. The commission found 528 Paiutes left in Utah and suggested that they be moved to the Moapa Reservation, in nearby Nevada. Such a move was thought necessary, because the situation of the Paiutes was becoming more and more desperate. Certainly the impact of the settlers on the lives of the Paiutes was shattering. Their land was taken and their traditional sources of food depleted in less than twenty years. As they were incorporated into the Mormon and then the federal systems, their ability to feed themselves faltered, and they became progressively more dependent on the whites for their survival. After their land base was taken, they were no longer a military threat and were of little interest to the settler colonists. Jacob Hamlin, one of the men most responsible for the success of the Mormon colonizing effort in southern Utah, wrote to J. W. Powell, in 1880, that: "The watering places are all occupide {sic} by the white man. The grass that product mutch {sic} seed is all et {sic} out. The sunflowere seed is all distroyed [*sic*] in fact thare [*sic*] is nothing for them to depend upon but beg or starve" (Fowler and Fowler 1971:110).

Yet most of the Paiutes still did not move and were reduced to relying on Mormon welfare, odd jobs, and begging, until the establishment of the Shivwits Reservation, on the Santa Clara River, in 1891. Despite their ideological status as a chosen people, the Paiutes became a nuisance that the Mormons felt compelled to feed occasionally. The Indian Service found itself with insufficient funds or manpower to make a genuine effort to offer any coherent development plan to the tiny groups of Indian people scattered all over southern Utah. The earlier failure of the Senate to ratify the Paiute treaty meant that they had no treaty rights and were regarded for years as "scattered bands" and thus ineligible for substantial federal assistance. The decision to provide aid to only those Indians that regrouped on the reservations was to have far-ranging consequences for the scattered Paiutes.

The Bitter Years

The Indian Appropriation Act of 1871 ended treaty making between the United States and the various Indian tribes. With the end of the treaty-making system, influential members of Congress stated that the previous policy of treating the Indians as sovereign, yet dependent wards no longer made sense. This marked the end of negotiating with the tribes and the beginning of a period characterized by Congress's exercise of plenary power, as it decreed the fate of the Indian nations.

The period between 1874 and 1927 is one of the least-documented and most poorly understood in Paiute history. The riverine bands along the Santa Clara and the Virgin were virtually wiped out by disease, and the survivors were displaced from their traditional camping sites by Mormon towns and settlers. The misery of the surviving Paiutes is attested by letters, photographs, and oral histories.

During the early 1900s, the Paiutes were virtually ignored by the federal government. In 1912 the scattered bands in Utah were under the nominal supervision of Special Agent Lorenzo Creel, in Salt Lake City. Except for brief visits, however, the southern Paiutes were essentially unsupervised, until the Shivwits and the Cedar Band were placed under the supervision of the superintendent at Goshute Indian School, in 1916. The Goshute Reservation, at Ibapah, Utah, lies 210 miles west of Salt Lake City; Cedar City is 250 miles south of Salt Lake City. Any sustained activity by federal Indian agents in Utah was impossible, as they suffered from a lack of funds and personnel. The inability of government agents to significantly influence the Paiutes was exacerbated by the fact that the Indians were scattered about southern Utah in small clusters, far from a major BIA office. This neglect was reinforced by the assumption that Indians not confined to an approved reservation were either on their own or should rely on the local Mormons for any help that they might need.

The situation of the Southern Paiutes was bleak, and survival was difficult. For the remnants of the population that survived the initial white conquest, life centered around a cycle of intermittent wage labor, gleaning Mormon fields, some farming on tiny plots of land, and hunting. They hunted jackrabbits and prairie dogs for meat (Manning n.d.), earned some money picking fruit and grubbing stumps for the whites, and continued to gather some wild plant foods. Woolsey (1964), like so many of the local historians, mentions the women doing laundry, making baskets, tanning buckskins, and selling pine nuts, while the men chopped wood, worked in the whites' fields, and trapped coyotes and wildcats. Some Paiutes attached themselves to particular white farmers and worked for subsistence-level wages and/ or a small portion of what they harvested.

Pine nuts were especially important as a supplementary food supply and as a cash crop to be sold to the whites. Palmer (1936a) states that the Paiutes of Cedar City were often cheated by local white merchants, who paid them less per pound for their pine nuts than the announced price and charged them more for staples such as flour, sugar, and beans. Indian women worked as domestics, earning as much as $1.50 to $2.00 a day, while the men did farm work, stock raising, and common labor, such as grubbing stumps (Annual Report 1918). The Koosharem group raised its own grain and hay and worked in the beet fields in the spring and fall, earning as much as $2.00 a day (McConihe 1915). In September of 1927, Farrow reported that the Indians "have to gather pinenuts at this time of year in order to have sufficient money to carry them through the winter months . . ." (1927:2). At Indian Peaks the Paiutes cultivated twenty acres of lucern, corn, potatoes, melons, and other vegetables.

While the BIA did little during this period to improve Paiute economic conditions, it did begin to provide some education. Under the influence of the national reform movement, Bureau of Indian Affairs policy encouraged the establishment of educational institutions to provide a white-oriented education for Indian children.[1] The first day school for southern Paiutes was established in 1898, at Shivwits, and was known as the Shebit Day School. The report of Laura Work from the Shebit Day School, in 1899 (Work 1899:431–2), indicates that there had been a "terrible drought" and also a "great amount of sickness and alarming number of deaths." She also reported that the surrounding whites were stirring up the Indians by "exciting tales of prospective removals" and were "inciting the Indians to refuse to come here . . ." The records indicate that this school closed in 1903 and moved to Panguitch, as a boarding school. The federal government purchased the Haycock farm, three miles north of Panguitch, Utah, at Three Mile Creek. Here they established a Paiute boarding school that opened in September 1904. According to a locally produced history of Garfield County (Daughters of Utah Pioneers, 1949:240):

> The Indian Office in Washington, D.C., who had charge of it, enlarged the house, built dormitories for boys and girls, built large barns and other out-buildings, stocked the farm with milk cows, beef cattle, other livestock, farm implements, etc., and began a course of vocational, as well as educational work.

An old photograph shows thirty Indian children in uniforms, standing in front of the brick main house. Apparently the cold weather (due to the elevation of Panguitch), the location (at a distance from Paiute homes), the opposition of Indian parents, and Commissioner Leupp's tendency to reduce schools and services all contributed to the decision to close the Panguitch Indian Training School on June 30, 1909. The school was once again moved to Shivwits as a day school and continued as such until 1930.

By 1915 at Shivwits, the Indians made as much as $50 per family gathering pine nuts, and the BIA seemed primarily interested in the school and in assuring the quality of the agricultural products displayed at various fairs and fruit festivals (Wagner 1915).

William Manning (n.d.:12) described the way the Paiutes lived in the early 1920s in this manner:

> Each family lived in a little one room shack which was their kitchen, bed room, and living room. Around the walls ranged bed rolls in the day, and at night the floor was covered with beds especially if company came. Food was prepared on a small stove and eaten from a small table with the pot or frying pan set in the middle. Each helped himself out of the pot with his fingers, and sat on the floor, the room being too small for very many chairs.

Martha Knack (1986) has documented that some Paiutes in Nevada (doing wage labor on an Anglo-owned ranch) found themselves caught within a system of debt peonage. Wheat flour replaced ricegrass and other traditional foods, and their reliance on credit extended by their employers incorporated them into a system in which they could not become competitors; they were forced to remain landless employees. My older informants often mentioned their parents and grandparents doing wage labor for white farmers (the men grubbed stumps and the women washed clothes). These data suggest that by the early 1900s, the Utah Paiutes found themselves enmeshed in a wage-labor system that ensured that their status as laborers would remain static. These changes occurred concurrently with the Paiutes' loss of autonomy (Smith 1966:123) and their decline into a tiny, powerless minority.

The Trust Responsibility

During the early twentieth century, the federal government slowly began to affect the lives of Paiutes through its various Indian policies. This agonizingly sluggish process continued until, in the 1950s, it became the most important factor in deciding the affairs of the Paiute people. To a great extent, the negative effects of many ill-conceived federal policies have been a result of the basic assumption that, since the Indians are the wards of the government, Congress can do as it pleases to solve the "Indian problem." While the origins of the government's attitudes toward Native Americans lie deep in our colonial past, the modern doctrine was fully elucidated by U.S. Chief Justice John Marshall, in his famous decision on the *Cherokee Nation v. the State of Georgia,* handed down in 1831. Marshall's opinion described American Indians as "domestic dependent nations" that had, of their own volition, relinquished their power to regulate trade and make treaties to the United States. The argument of the time was that while the tribes retained rights as independent political powers, they were subordinate to the United States and were becoming dependent on the United States for their welfare and existence. The Indians had the right to occupy their lands only until the federal government chose to extinguish their title. "Meanwhile they are in a state of pupilage; their relationship to the United States resembles that of a ward to his guardian" (Marshall, quoted in Canby 1981:34). The key word here is "resembles," because while the trust relationship resembles wardship, the Indians are not under legal guardianship (L. Cohen 1960:328–34), although they are the recipients of special rights.

The keystone of Indian trust-relationship rights is the safeguarding of Indian land and property. Beyond the management and protection of Indian land and water rights, the boundaries of trust responsibility are vague. According to Prucha (1986:399), Indians and their advocates generally argue for a broad interpretation of the trust responsibility that includes "education, health care and other social services." Historically the BIA has attempted to deliver these services, and most Native Americans have grown to expect them as part of the trustee's responsibility. However broadly interpreted, this fiduciary relationship is a moral and a legal one, based on treaty and other rights, but is not enforceable against the desires of Congress (Canby 1981:35). Much of the character of federal paternalism stems from Congress's changing interpretation of this trust responsibility, resulting in a cycle of contradictory policies.

Not only did the courts and "common wisdom" view Indians as politically and economically dependent; they were also seen as morally dependent. Thus part of the "white man's burden" consisted of civilizing the Native American. Here the viewpoints of the Mormons, other religious denominations, the U.S. Congress, and private citizens converged. The fact that many tribes were being impoverished by the tide of Anglo settlers, rather than by their own incompetence, was seldom articulated. It was the end result of the white land grabbing that created public opinion; the Indians were becoming dependent on the government for their subsistence. This dependency reinforced the image of the Anglo as benevolent parent and of the Indian as wayward child.

Reservations by Executive Order

The trust responsibility has generally been implemented by the federal government, through the Bureau of Indian Affairs, on reservations and through reservation-based programs. By the time the BIA attempted to fulfill the trust obligations to the Paiutes, the federal government was trying to get out of the reservation business. This was the period when Congress's favored policy was allotment: the breakup of tribal identities and land bases.

The four tiny reservations that became the homes of the surviving Paiutes were established between the years 1891 and 1929, by executive order. Thus the Paiute reservations were created at the same time that Congress was attempting to implement a policy of abolishing reservations. Not surprisingly the Paiute reservations were small and were comprised of little productive land and few water rights. In addition help from the BIA was sporadic and of little consequence to the daily lives of the Paiutes.

SHIVWITS

The presence of Paiutes in northern Arizona created problems for Mormon colonists, who then appealed to the government for help. The establishment of the first Paiute reservation, at Shivwits (near St. George, Utah), was the result of the initiative of an individual Mormon and the ensuing federal response to his proposal. The account of Anthony Ivins (n.d.) details this interaction:

> The writer, soon after he acquired the interests of the Mohave Company and added to the number of company cattle his own herd, which he had grazed on the Trumbull Mountain [in northern Arizona]. It at once became evident that ranching could not

be successfully carried on while the Shevwits remained on the land, the right to which they had sold to others (Mohave Land and Cattle Company). They became insolent, frequently killed cattle for food, and when remonstrated with replied that the country was theirs, and that the white man, with his flocks and herds, should move away, and leave them in peaceful possession.

Representation was made to the Indian department, at Washington, and the suggestion offered that the Shevwits be removed to a reservation on the Santa Clara River [in southern Utah], where they would be among civilized people, and subject to proper government supervision. The suggestion was approved, funds were appropriated for the purchase and improvement of the land, and the writer was appointed to establish an agency, and place the Shevwits upon it (see also Ivins 1916).

Although the Shivwits had "sold" the rights to springs and water holes to the white cattle company, they obviously did not think that this "sale" extinguished all rights to their homeland. When Ivins found them in his way, he utilized federal channels to remove the Paiutes from their homeland, for "their own good." This paternalism lasted for only two years, as Ivins served as Indian Agent from 1891 to 1893. His reputation was, however, established as a "friend of the Indian."

Shivwits reservation was established in 1891, with a congressional appropriation of $40,000 (see figure 3). President Woodrow Wilson issued an executive order, in 1916, which expanded the size of the reservation to 26,880 acres. The small Indian school was established there and the school superintendent then acted as agent for the government.

INDIAN PEAKS

The Indian Peaks Reservation was established by executive order on August 2, 1915, and was enlarged in 1921, 1923, and 1924. The reservation was 10,240 acres of rough, rocky land, mostly covered with juniper, but yielding large quantities of pine nuts in a good year. The Indian Peaks Band was a composite group, formed from the remnants of several other groups, including the Paragoon, Pahquit, and Tavatsock bands (Palmer 1946a). One informant suggested that the Paiutes

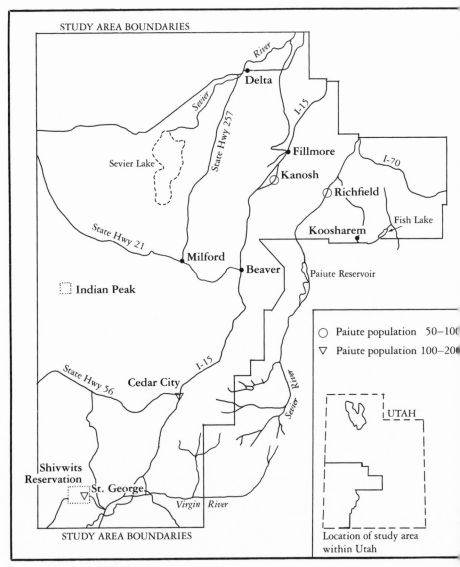

Figure 3. *Southern Paiute Reservations and Population Centers*

were moved to Indian Peaks by a federal Indian agent from Salt Lake City named Quail and then abandoned; I have been unable to verify this report (Holt fieldnotes 1982). The Paiutes living at Indian Peaks were the last to avoid becoming dependent on the whites. They raised vegetables and animals and gathered pine nuts. They lived in five log houses, forty-five miles northwest of Lund, Utah, which was the nearest post office (Palmer 1936a:6).

K O O S H A R E M

A reservation was established for the Koosharem band of Utes in 1928; it was later enlarged, in 1937. These people were probably the remnants of the Fish Lake Utes, a culturally transitional group between the Utes and the Paiutes. They considered themselves to be Utes, but made fewer of the changes from the prehorse Basin culture than did other Utes. The Koosharem group ranged from Fish Lake, in the summer, to the environs of present-day Escalante, in the winter.

The Koosharem people were under the control of the local Mormon church (Sevier Stake), which was also trustee of their water rights, until the Paiutes sued for those rights, in 1958. This band eventually became dependent on the town of Richfield. The Koosharem people did seasonal work in the beet and other fields surrounding Richfield, which was the largest town in this part of Utah; the original site at Koosharem offered almost no wage labor.

K A N O S H

The last reservation to be formally established in Utah was the Kanosh Reservation, established in February 1929 and expanded in 1935 and 1937. The Kanosh band members were descended from the Pahvant Indians, who inhabited the Corn Creek region in the early historic period. Palmer (1936b) states that they also incorporated the remnants of three other groups. A letter in the *Deseret News* of 13 December 1851 stated that the Pah-van-te Indians "reside upon Corn Creek . . . and have there raised corn, beans, pumpkins, squashes, potatoes, etc., year after year, for a period that dates further back than their acquaintance with the whites." When Palmer visited them in 1935, he noted twenty-three members of the band, living in five houses. He reported that their agricultural production had fallen since 1930, when they had lost about half the water rights they had held between 1853 and 1930 "through some arrangements made through the Indian agent" (Palmer 1936a). Palmer states, "The chief tells me that the 'Whites' were angry and jealous every time they had to buy something from the Indians and they said the Indians had more water than they needed" (1936a). Several attempts had been made earlier to remove the Pahvant, who shared both Ute and Paiute cultural characteristics, to the Uintah Reservation. However the Pahvant, like the Paiutes to the south, refused to leave their homeland. One white informant suggested that the Kanosh group claimed they were Paiutes in order to avoid being shipped to the Uintah and Ouray reservations, but I have not been able to confirm this view. They did, however, tend to marry Paiutes, so that their "Paiuteness" increased through both genetic relationships and cultural sharing.

The Kanosh Pahvant reservation, like the Koosharem Ute/Paiute reservation, was administered by the BIA office that was established in Cedar City in 1927. The band gradually came to be considered Paiute, as an administrative convenience. In 1990 the Kanosh group, and to a lesser extent the Koosharem group, still considered themselves to be more Ute, and thus superior to other Paiutes.

THE CEDAR CITY FIASCO

The final group of what was to become the Utah Paiutes survived white contact by amalgamating in a small ghetto in Cedar City. Federal funds had been appropriated in 1899 to buy land for the Cedar City group, but, for unknown reasons, no land was ever purchased and the money was returned to surplus.

The Cedar City Paiutes had lost all their land to settlers and were classified as a "scattered band" by the Indian Service. From 1912 to 1916 they were nominally administered by Lorenzo Creel from Salt Lake City, 250 miles to the north. At least one agent, W. W. McConihe, visited Cedar City, in 1915, and suggested that eighty acres be purchased, at fifteen hundred dollars, for the use of the Paiutes (McConihe

1915). But when Lorenzo Creel was informed by the commissioner of Indian affairs that there were no funds available for purchase of lands for Utah Indians, he stated "that this matter of buying land and building houses be closed for the present. . . . I have made repeated efforts to find land on the Public Domain for them, but have been unable to do so as they desire to remain in the vicinity in which they now live" (Creel 1916:1).

Available records suggest that even the most marginal supervision of the Cedar City Paiutes did not begin until the establishment of an agency at Goshute, far to the north, in 1916. The early location of the Paiutes in Cedar City seems to have been on eleven acres, west of Interstate Highway 15 (near the present Coleman Company). This land was apparently traded to a white for horses and perhaps a wagon (Holt fieldnotes, Matheson interview, August 20, 1982; Palmer 1946a). At a later date, they were moved to another tract of land, comprising about five acres, near the present baseball park, by the LDS Relief Society, which retained title to the land. In 1919 the Cedar City Paiutes were administered as a "scattered band," from the Goshute Reservation. They had the use of eighty acres of land for farming, plus the five and one-half acres they lived on. The Goshute superintendent (Annual Report 1919:1–2) reported that:

I found that the people of this vicinity were interested in these people and spoke in high praise of them, as being industrious and sober.

Their homes are very crude and unsanitary and should be improved by the addition of eight cottages and connection with the city water mains. . . . Fourteen persons ate and slept in one house, 14×18 feet in dimensions, during the winter of 1918–19, and the same conditions will prevail this winter unless they are given some assistance in getting better homes. . . . Their homes are mere hovels, and old and wornout tents, and one or two old women were living under some old ragged canvass spread over a large clump of sage brush. They seem very much attached to the locality and would not consider or entertain a proposition to remove to the Goshute Indian Reserve, or to Indian Peak.

In 1924 attempts were made to drive the Paiutes from the "shacks" that were so squalid and unhealthy that several people had died in the past years from tuberculosis. A Mormon church plan to move and rehouse the group was outlined at a meeting of the Cedar City Chamber of Commerce by William Palmer (president of the Parowan Stake). The plan envisioned moving the Paiutes:

> . . . to a plot of ground further north than where they are at present situated. He [Palmer] said that an effort had been made to get the U.S. Government to take hold of the matter, but all the government could do was to have them go to some Indian reservation, this being against the desires of the Indians. (Iron County Record 1924)

The government began to act to help the Cedar band, but it acted very slowly. On March 2, 1925, an act (43 Stat. 1096) authorized the appropriation of $1275 for the purchase of nine lots in Cedar City. Two months later William Palmer wrote an article for a local paper, saying that the government refused to do anything for the Paiutes:

> Men who had the welfare of both races at heart, sensing that an early action was imperative, laid the pitiable conditions of the Indians of Cedar before the Mormon Church and appealed to them to reach out the strong arm of sympathy and relief, which the government has withheld. (Iron County Record 1925)

The Mormon church proceeded with a removal plan, and on December 25, 1926, they were moved to the property purchased for them by the church (which retained the title to the land). Their old camp, shacks, and belongings were burned. Palmer (1946a) stated that: "After several months time during which presumably, Dr. Farrow was in communication with the Department of Indian affairs in Washington, D.C., he reported back that nothing could be done 'because this was a roving band of Indians.'"

Although it is not clear whether Farrow was in communication with Palmer about the 1925 appropriation, he reported both the appropriation and the Mormon land purchase so matter-of-factly that one is led to believe that he was aware of it. Farrow reported the purchase to the commissioner of Indian affairs, stating that: "It would appear that no further action on our part is warranted . . . and I believe that no action looking towards an appropriation for the proposed purchase need be made" (Butler 1965). Explaining his actions in a letter to the CIA, Farrow said:

> I recommended that the appropriation be allowed to lapse in-
> asmuch as it was not likely that the Indians would ever return
> to the old tract, the health authorities having destroyed their
> huts, and there was a certain amount of local opposition to the
> re-establishment of the camp at the old site. (Farrow 1930)

The money was appropriated and was finally carried to surplus in fiscal year 1928 (Butler 1965). Cedar City was not part of Farrow's administrative duties, but his acting as the de facto representative of the government may have influenced his being chosen to head a new agency in Cedar City.

The Allotment Policy

In his 1889 report, the commissioner of Indian affairs, T. Morgan, referred to the Indian reservation as a "legalized reformatory" for Indians. From the days of Thomas Jefferson, the "Indian question" had been one of determining the quickest and least expensive method of educating and assimilating the Indians into the mainstream culture: to turn them into taxpayers rather than dependent wards (Sheehan 1973:89–116). The major contradiction underlying the creation and application of various federal Indian policies was the drive for posses-sion of Indian land and resources. Federal paternalism was constantly constrained and shaped by white images of the Indian (Berkhofer 1979) and the pressure of settlers for more cheap land. Indian reservations were the last substantial source of land for the greedy newcomers.

Prucha (1986:198–99) has suggested that the 1880s and 1890s were the high point of paternalism, as Christian reformers and "friends of the Indians" attempted to turn Native Americans away from tribal-ism and their native religions and assimilate them as patriotic, individualistic American citizens. The reformers felt that this goal could best be accomplished through education and the end of the reservation system. Federal, state, and local laws and authority were to be extended to the tribes, and what remained of their communal sovereignty was to be extinguished. Ending the tribal/communal systems of land tenure associated with the reservations would enable the Indians to become independent farmers. Thus for paternalistic reformers and greedy speculators alike, the obvious solution to tribalism and the desire for cheap land was to break up the reservations and give each Indian a tiny homestead. After each head of an Indian family had been allotted 160 acres, there would still be millions of acres available for white use.

A fundamental tenet of allotment was that the reservation system and tribalism were responsible for the poverty and lack of assimilation of the Indian peoples into the national culture. The allotment of tribal land began when Congress passed the Indian Homestead Act, in 1875. A number of other allotment bills were submitted to Congress in the 1880s. As usual in Indian affairs, there were two perspectives: the gradual approach and the immediate approach. The gradual approach to assimilation was championed by Senator Henry Dawes, who favored a gradual allotment process. Others, including many of the reformers, land speculators, and homesteaders favored the immediate allotment of all reservation land.

The conflicting views as to the speed of assimilation resulted in a compromise bill, the Dawes Severalty Act of 1887. This act was the first in a series of federal policies designed to make Indians independent that would actually increase the dependence of the vast majority of Native Americans on the federal government. The theory behind the Dawes Act was that once an individual Indian became a private property holder, he would then automatically desire and acquire the other middle-class characteristics he had previously lacked. The peak of land acquisition through the Homestead Act had occurred in 1884. In 1881 Senator George Pendleton summed up the goals of the Dawes Act: "It means the allotment of these tribal lands to the individual; it means to encourage the idea of property; it means to encourage the idea of home; it means to encourage the idea of family; it tends to break up the tribe" (Tyler 1964:4).

Indian lands were divided up into individual plots; after an initial twenty-five year "trust" period, they became liable to taxation. Lands declared "surplus" would then be sold to whites. By 1934 the tribal land base had been reduced by eighty-six million acres through white acquisition. Instead of making the Indians independent private-property holders (its avowed purpose) the act, in general, increased the state of Indian poverty and dependence by reducing their resource base and their access to meaningful federal help.

Allotment and The Paiutes

Prior to the passage of the Dawes Act, in 1887, allotments were made (apparently as part of the Indian Homestead Act or the other experiments that had preceded the Dawes Act) for both the Koosharem and the Kanosh people. As with most federal policies, the effects of the Dawes Act on the Paiutes were the opposite of those intended by Congress. At Koosharem 400 acres of land, in three allotments, were patented in 1904 and 1913. The 1904 patent was issued to Walker Kisalve, with the assistance of the local Mormon church. The Mormon church filed for six homesteads in 1900, under the 1884 act, and later the Kanosh Indians received 1,840 acres of land in twelve allotments, in 1919 and 1920.[2] These allotments at Koosharem and Kanosh served as the core of Indian-owned land, around which these Ute/Paiutes could organize their work and other activities. The allotments also served to mark land for potential Indian ownership; when the reservations were established at Koosharem and at Kanosh, they were adjacent to the allotments. Allotment gave them land where before they had had only squatters' rights. Not only were the allotments useful in creating an owned core of land, they also forced local whites to allocate water rights. Thus instead of helping to break up the tribe, as Congress had intended, allotments in the Paiute case tended to preserve the separate identity of the Indians.

Mormon Prejudice and Neglect

The early missionary concern of the 1850s for the Lamanites seems by the early twentieth century to have been replaced by a feeling of extreme prejudice. Whites around the Shivwits Reservation reportedly did not care "to intermingle with the Indians, in any way except work . . ." (U.S. BIA Annual Report Paiute-Goshute 1917). The local Mormons were generally ready to feed the occasional Indian who might happen by, but were more interested in the economic survival of their small farms and businesses than in the uplifting of the Lamanite. The Koosharem group seems to have been under the strictest control of the local Mormons. Special Indian Agent McConihe noted that the Mormons around Koosharem "take a kindly interest in these Indians and the Bishop and Mr. Hatch, look after their interests very closely and the Indians seem to have every confidence in them" (1915:1). Tolerance toward the Indians lasted as long as they kept in their place. Woolsey relates that a Paiute in Escalante, during the winter of 1910, entered a dance hall carrying a dead eagle. He rebuked the whites, saying:

My friends it is right for white man to have celebration, to talk about land—white man land—white man flag—big United States. White man money—dollar—has eagle on one side. White man like eagle, big bird. Today I find eagle, white boy shoot— holds up eagle—dead now—maybe so last one, last eagle, no more eagle. One time many eagle (pointing toward cliffs). Too much shoot. Indian shoot little bit. White man shoot too much. Eagle all gone.

Maybe so pretty soon, Indian all gone. One time many Indian. Many papoose. Now Indian die. Papoose die. Sleep in cave (pointing to hills). Indian sleep. Little bit food. One time much rabbit, much fish, much deer. Now little bit. White man give Indian bread. Indian beg. Squaw beg 'Give bread.' No good. Indian no like beg.

Me Indian chief (gestures to indicate head dress with feathers, then to pull it off.) Now me no chief. No good! No good! Papoose too much die. Eagle all gone. Pretty soon Indian all gone. (1964:384)

Mormon efforts to aid the Paiutes were sporadic and disorganized. William Manning was the director of the music department at the

Branch Agricultural College (later Southern Utah State College); he organized an "Indian Show," in order to raise money to buy blankets and clothing to replace that which had been burned when the Cedar City Paiutes were moved from their camp by the baseball park to their current location to the north. Manning invited President Ivins and Utah Governor George Dern down to see the act and be initiated into the Paiutes tribe. On the third night of the performance, May 11, 1926, William Palmer was initiated. Manning's show raised $500 for the Paiutes (Manning n.d.). In the eyes of the Mormon church, William Palmer emerged from this episode a clear winner; as an honorary member of the Cedar band, he emerged as the principal white mediator with the Paiutes. His association with the Paiutes allowed him a strong channel of communication with Anthony Ivins (who became member of the First Council of the Seventy) and the church leaders, in Salt Lake City.

Local individuals such as Manning and Palmer played an important role as mediators between the Paiutes and the local white population. Not only did they act as liaisons between the two populations, they also acted as advisors and assumed the role of the local "friend of the Indian." They were the individuals to whom the Paiutes came when they were in need of food or other essentials or when they had problems with the police, courts, or individual whites. Between 1900 and 1949, Mormon church missionary work with the Paiutes was spotty and inconsistent and depended on the individual efforts of men like Manning.[3] Such individuals, through actions designed to help the Paiutes, personified the ideology of paternalism. A Mormon Paiute informant explained the role of the white leader by saying:

> Once you have a leader that knows how to handle the Indians' culture and tries to make them become educated, religious, and nice—once that person is gone, then the Indian people are left on their own and its hard for them not to have a leader to tell them what to do all the time. . . . It takes a certain type of person to know their lifestyle and their background—the problems dealing with alcohol mostly. (Holt fieldnotes, Growler interview, January 15, 1983)

Employment for the Paiutes remained intermittent, and this is a key element in their particular dependent relationship with the whites. Their labor was only necessary at particular times, such as harvesting; the rest of the year, they survived by doing odd jobs, hunting and gathering, and collecting welfare from the Mormons. The Paiutes adapted to Mormon paternalism, and it became an important resource within their changed environment. It is important to note, however, that Mormon aid was always in the form of wages or food, i.e., consumables, never capital. They were fed but never given a vehicle for raising themselves to the whites' standard of living.

The Paiute Agency

On January 1, 1927, the Bureau of Indian Affairs consolidated several offices and put six small reservations and four Indian settlements under the jurisdiction of a Paiute agency, located at Cedar City. The agency superintendent was Dr. E. A. Farrow, who had previously worked at the Kaibab Paiute Reservation, just across the Utah border, in northern Arizona. Farrow administered 393 "reservation" Indians and 103 Indians classified as members of "scattered bands." In 1932 the agency staff consisted of two Indian policemen and twelve white employees: the superintendent and a financial clerk in Cedar City, three teachers, two school housekeepers, one farm agent, two farmers, and two stockmen.

The presence of a Paiute agency in Cedar City did little for the Cedar City Paiutes. In 1930 Farrow stated:

Having obtained an office ruling based on a decision of the Comptroller General that Indians allied with no tribe and having no trust property could not partake of the benefits of appropriations made for support and civilization of Indians, we have consistently taken the stand that the strictly Cedar City Indians were nonwards, at least from the standpoint of finances. As a physician I have given them all possible assistance and have been mediator in their local troubles. The care and upkeep of the property on which they live has been left entirely to the church authorities. (Farrow 1930:1–2)

Later in this letter, referring to Paiutes from Indian Peaks coming to
live with the Cedar band, Farrow wrote:

> The peculiar condition that exists with a mixture of undoubted
> wards temporarily living with Indians who are non-wards has
> caused considerable confusion and many misunderstandings on
> the part of the Indians and the whites. It is my opinion that as
> long as the Cedar City band elect to remain upon the land set aside
> for them by an organization other than the federal government
> that they should be deemed non-wards and dropped entirely from
> the rolls of this jurisdiction. (Farrow 1930:2)

Thus the inability of the federal government to deal with groups
such as the Paiutes led individuals within the LDS church to help the
Paiutes by securing more substantial housing (and, of course, ridding
their white neighbors of the Indian nuisance). In the convoluted logic
of the BIA at that time, the fact that they were on private land under
the control of the Mormon church meant that they were ineligible for
federal help.

In 1930 BIA services to Utah Indians were extremely limited, and
the reservations were not productive enough to provide all the residents with an adequate living. A Bureau report noted that the resources of the "reserves are so limited, the Indian groups so small
in numbers and parts of the population so nomadic in character on
account of the necessity of moving about in search of work" (U.S. BIA
Annual Report of the Board of Indian Commissioners 1931). This report also noted the lack of interest in Indian affairs on the part of the
local communities and the uncertainty of state officials "as to where
wardship rules are to begin and end." The report concluded that the
scattered bands of "primitive nomads will eventually 'die out.' And
that efforts should be made to have these smaller bands 'looked after'
by the local authorities . . . rather than an Indian agent located at some
distant point." During this period the "local authorities" were the local
bishops of the Mormon church; they considered the local Indians to be
their wards and often resented the sporadic visits of the BIA.

The Indian New Deal

The Dawes Act was finally considered to have been a failure with the release of the Meriam report in 1928. In *The Problem of Indian Administration*, Lewis Meriam and his associates recommended the ending of allotments and emphasized that the role of the BIA should primarily be one of education. Regarding allotment, the report stated that:

> Part of the plan was to instruct and aid them in agriculture, but this vital part was not pressed with vigor and intelligence. It almost seems as if the government assumed that some magic in individual ownership of property would in itself prove an educational civilizing factor, but unfortunately this policy has for the most part operated in the opposite direction. (Meriam 1928:7)

As Tyler explains (1973:123–24), the Meriam report laid the foundation upon which the Indian Reorganization Act was built; but the Great Depression, with its associated economic and political upheaval, was the moving force.

In October 1929 the stock market suffered a serious decline and fell to a low point in 1933. By then the American banking system had virtually collapsed. The country elected a new president in 1932; Franklin Roosevelt was inaugurated in March 1933 and began a series of unprecedented government interventions in the national economy. These programs were collectively known as the "New Deal."

The Paiutes and the Depression

For many Indians the depression years were a relatively good period. There was more aid available and federal jobs pumped money into the reservations. Although there were some federal projects on the Shivwits, Indian Peaks, and Kanosh reservations and the Paiutes participated in several federal works projects, the overall economic condition of the Paiutes improved at a very slow pace in the 1930s. Paiutes participated in WPA and IECW projects; for many of the Utah Paiutes, the relief agencies provided their first dependable incomes as they were hired for WPA projects and farm work. The Bureau of Indian

Affairs Annual Narrative Reports between 1932 and 1936 indicate that some agricultural and employment progress was made by the Paiutes during these years. In 1936 it was estimated that the average yearly income per family was between $150 and $200 at Shivwits. At Kanosh family earnings from pine nuts, farming, wood hauling, and wage labor were estimated at $200 in 1936 (U.S. BIA Findings and Recommendations 1936). From the sketchy records it appears that Kanosh and Shivwits benefited the most from the work programs, with Indian Peaks in third place. Very little seems to have happened at Koosharem. The 1936 BIA Annual Report states that: "The Koosharem Indians have been a great problem in this Agency. While they have a mental development and general economic status far below the average, their health conditions have been particularly good." The report further states that "the greater portion of their income is obtained from work done in the community. They seem to like to work for other people rather than plan and operate their own farms" (1936:n.p.). The report fails to mention that given the land, water, and financial resources of the Koosharem band, operating their own farms would have meant disaster.

The depression brought at least one Mormon church–sponsored project to the Paiutes: a church president gave William Palmer $500 to develop an arts and crafts business for the Paiutes. Articles such as baskets, gloves, moccasins, beaded bookends, and bows and arrows were produced for sale to tourists and local whites. Palmer (1936a) stated that: "During these times when there has been no work for them, this bit of employment has gone far toward supplying actual living necessities. They know that the church has furnished this money and they are grateful to them for it." Palmer said that by reinvesting the original $500, he was able to provide $1107 worth of employment in approximately one year.

The Indian Reorganization Act

As part of his new approach, President Roosevelt named a reformer, John Collier, to be the commissioner of Indian affairs. Realizing that reform had to touch every aspect of the relationship between the Indians and the federal government, Collier began to push vigorously for the reorganization of all relevant institutions. The key legislative element of John Collier's tenure as commissioner was the Indian Reorganization Act (Wheeler-Howard Act), or IRA (Philip 1977). The IRA not only repealed the Dawes Act and officially ended the practice of allotment, it also encouraged tribal self-government (within the limits of tribal constitutions and with the approval of the secretary of the interior; see Kelly 1975, Taylor 1980, Crum 1983), protected their remaining lands, and allowed for the purchase of new land. For many Native American groups, the Wheeler-Howard Act brought significant reforms and much-needed federal help.

Only two of the Paiute groups accepted the IRA: the Kanosh and Shivwits bands. In April 1935 F. A. Gross, the superintendent at the Ft. Hall Agency, and Dr. E. A. Farrow visited the various Paiute bands. In his report Gross stated that the Indians were in favor of the IRA everywhere except Cedar City:

It is believed that unless a radical change takes place between now and the time these people vote they will vote against the law or not vote at all. This group listened to the explanation of the law very courteously and patiently, but after the explanation had been made they indicated that they were not interested; that they did not wish to come under the law; that they had been getting along for many years without much help from the Government. (Gross 1935:1–2)

Perhaps it is indicative of Farrow's neglect of the Cedar City Paiute that the only negative comments on the IRA came from the band that lived in the city in which the Paiute Agency was located! According to Gross's report, the Koosharem band was in favor of the IRA; however, the only other mention of them in connection with the IRA seems to be in a report of an IRA committee, which stated that:

The committee was informed that most of the Indians enrolled there [Koosharem] were away gathering pine nuts and further realizing that these Indians are more or less a transitory group, the committee recommends that organization be delayed until such time that these few Indians have been rehabilitated. (U.S. BIA Indian Reorganization Act Committee 1936:22)

Thus the Koosharem group was left in the hands of the Mormon church for purposes of "rehabilitation." This action exemplifies the negative policy often adopted by the BIA during this period regarding the Paiutes; when in doubt, let the Mormon church handle the problem. The Koosharem band's water rights had been under the control of the Sevier Stake of the Mormon church since the early 1900s (Bagley 1926); in 1958 they sued the church, and the rights to their water were conveyed to their ownership. The majority of the Koosharem band settled at the Richfield "Indian village," near the light plant. This land was leased to the Sevier Stake of the Mormon church in 1969 for ten dollars, "for the sole and only purpose of providing dwelling places and garden plots for the Indian race, as the Leasee may see fit . . ." (Sorensen Lease 1969).

The situation of the Indian Peaks group during the 1930s is unclear; however, they came to be more closely identified with the Cedar City group, as they began to spend more time in Cedar City and less time on their desolate reservation. In 1935 Palmer (1936a) observed that the remaining eight Indian Peak residents were cultivating about ten acres and were being employed by the government to fence their reservation, in order to keep white livestock out. During the 1940s the Indian Peaks band moved into Cedar City, mostly living in the Indian village.

Kanosh and Shivwits under the IRA

At Kanosh the Indians earned an annual income per family of about $200, by engaging in farming, gathering pine nuts, hauling wood, and working for local whites at such wage labor as farming and road work; they also participated in relief job programs (Findings and Recommendations 1936:17).

The Shivwits Reservation consisted of 26,800 acres, of which only about 83 acres was ever cultivated. In 1936 lack of water prevented the Shivwits from planting the 70 acres that they normally cultivated. The rest of the reservation was grazing land, covered with brush, juniper grasses, and creosote (White 1946b:22). The eighty-one inhabitants of the reservation gathered pine nuts and performed wage labor, yielding family incomes of from $150 to $200 per year (U.S. BIA Findings and Recommendations 1936:11). The report of the Reorganization Committee concluded:

> It is apparent that additional farm land with ample irrigation water would be desirable for the Indians of this reservation.
>
> From the observations made by the committee it is quite evident that at the present time the Indians of this reservation are not in a position to act intelligently in participating in organization. (U.S. BIA Indian Reorganization Act Committee 1936:12)

The Kanosh group voted to accept the IRA on May 7, 1935, and the Shivwits followed on November 17, 1935. Although the efforts expended by the BIA for the IRA bands were entirely too little, available documents suggest that efforts were much more intense in the post-IRA era, and that the IRA groups among the Paiute fared far better than their non-IRA cousins. At Kanosh, for example, during the 1930s and 1940s, the government purchased $23,777.56 worth of land and expended $25,750.89 for new ditches and the development of the irrigation system (Stone 1951b).

For the first time, the two bands found themselves with a constitution and by-laws and leaders with both authority and responsibility. While they functioned with more recognized corporate authority (Smith 1966) than did their non-IRA cousins, consensus-based politics remained in force, and the tribal business councils displayed little initiative, preferring to follow the advice of BIA agents and the local Mormon mediators. They were only nominally autonomous under their IRA charters, however, and some of the simplest decisions, such as what and how much to plant, were made by BIA officials. Over one-half of the constitutional powers of the tribes under the IRA were subject to approval or review of the secretary of the interior (Barsh and Henderson 1980:117). The IRA, like the Allotment Act, was another policy failure for the government; again the results of the IRA were often the reverse of those intended.

While the IRA signified a greater involvement of the federal government in the affairs of the Southern Paiutes, there were few tangible results. The Act was instrumental, however, in bringing some obvious economic benefits to the Kanosh group and the Shivwits people; the other groups were totally bypassed by the Indian New Deal. This lack of progress under the IRA left the Paiutes in a very vulnerable position during the termination years that followed.

On the positive side, participation in IRA governments did give the Paiutes their first taste of western-style meetings, with their minutes, committee procedures, and majority-rule decision making. The IRA gave the Paiutes their first opportunity to work under parliamentary procedure and to cast their first votes. New leaders began to emerge, who blended the old search for consensus with the idea of majority rule. Instead of pushing the Paiutes toward assimilation, the IRA began the process of arming them with legal and organizational weapons they could use to protect their separate identity.

In the Shadow of the IRA

During the 1940s Paiute labor still played a minor role in Anglo agricultural practices, especially during harvesting.[4] In 1940 more than 68 percent of working Native Americans were engaged in agricultural work (Olson and Wilson 1984:185). World War II pushed Indian affairs to a new low on the list of federal priorities, and documents that include references to the Paiutes during the war years are rare and generally uninformative.

One IRA program that benefited both Shivwits and Kanosh was the revolving credit plan. J. E. White's credit report of 1946 listed nineteen families living at Shivwits, eight of whom occupied tents; he recommended that the Shivwits be given a $10,000 loan under the revolving credit plan (White 1946b). He noted (1946c:25) that the Shivwits band had $400 in the Bank of St. George and $1300 in liabilities (a note at the same bank). White's figures (1946b:31) indicate that the average family yearly income was $1688.[5] White (1946b:22) estimated that the carrying capacity of the Shivwits range lands was 130 cattle and horses. The record is unclear as to what became of the $10,000 loan to Shivwits, although some farm improvements were made (White 1946b).

The various BIA schemes for Shivwits never materialized. In 1949 it became apparent that the Shivwits Tribal Corporation could neither meet its payments to the revolving credit fund nor make a profit, given its resources. Not only were the Paiutes' resource bases on their small reservations too small to support even their tiny population, but their credit, farm implements, and training were inadequate to provide for self-sufficiency. The BIA, like the Mormons, only gave them enough to get by, never enough to really raise their standard of living.

The Shivwits Reservation was eventually leased to a white for an annual payment of $2000 plus water assessments (Stone 1951b). This marked the end of farming (other than small, individual gardens) at Shivwits and illustrates the failure of the IRA-based policy to turn the Paiutes into an independent farming people.

Another $10,000 revolving-credit loan to Kanosh (only that amount was advanced, although a total of $25,000 was approved) apparently only cancelled the debts of the Kanosh Farm Enterprise, since their commercial debts totaled at least $8,500 (White 1946a). Again the loan only allowed them to function at the same level and did little to help them develop their infrastructure.

In March of 1946, the Kanosh Reservation consisted of 7,729.5 acres; it had been enlarged by 4,050 acres, as a result of purchases authorized under the IRA, in 1936 and 1937. These lands were acquired at a cost to the government of about $23,777. An additional 600 acres were assigned to them from the public domain, in 1944. In the report of Credit Agent White (1946a), average annual family income was listed as $1,014.75 in 1945. About 28 percent of this income came from Social Security temporary assistance and pensions. The Kanosh Reservation, after the additions made possible by the IRA, was a viable farming operation, and White recommended that credit of $10,000 be extended to the Kanosh band from the Indian Service Revolving Credit fund. The Kanosh farming operation was the most successful of all the Paiute attempts to create a comfortable lifestyle based on agriculture. As we shall see in the next chapter, this venture was destroyed by the policy of termination.

3 THE AGONY
of
TERMINATION

FEDERAL INDIAN POLICY after World War II focused on job placement and relocation of Indians to urban areas, Indian claims, and the termination of trust status for Indian tribes. During this period a conservative consensus emerged in Congress and began to emphasize its plenary power over Indian affairs (Barsh and Henderson 1980:112–34). Returning warriors found times hard in Indian country. Vine Deloria and Clifford Lytle (1984:190) characterize these decades between 1945 and 1965 as "the barren years."

The central concept that drove federal policy during these years was termination, the essential ingredient of which was the revocation of the trust relationship between the government and the tribes. The legal lineage of the termination policy can easily be traced as far back as the formative ideas of the Dawes Allotment Act of 1887: that tribalism was the major stumbling block to the assimilation of Indians into the mainstream, and that Indians should not be treated differently from any other citizens. Although the 1928 Meriam report (Tyler 1964:13–15) recommended that states assume responsibility for Indian affairs other than property-related issues, the real push for withdrawal of federal trust responsibility coincided with anti-BIA sentiments in Congress and the intent of Congress to keep the postwar budget trimmed.

There was a consensus in Congress during the late 1940s that the BIA was one of the most ineffective federal agencies and that the IRA was a failure because it sheltered Indians from their responsibilities as Americans. The promises of the IRA had, indeed, remained un-fulfilled, since Indians were never given the resources or backing by Congress to insure even a modicum of success. Termination as a policy alternative gained support after 1945, because the Indian Reorgani-zation Act, the centerpiece of John Collier's Indian New Deal, had failed "to solve the problems associated with the previous policy of assimilation and land allotment" (Philp 1983:169).

Congress also failed to realize the impact of World War II on the reservations (Deloria and Lytle 1984:190–93), as the federal govern-ment's funds and attention were focused on the war and not on Native Americans. From the perspective of supporters of Indian assimilation, Collier's policies were seen as an aberration, in that they had per-petuated the reservations and had strengthened both Indian cultural awareness and tribal government.

The Roots of Termination

Congressional animosity toward the Bureau of Indian Affairs, which had been exiled to Chicago during World War II, had grown to the point where the Bureau was seen as the worst and most inefficient agency of the federal government. When termination was first dis-cussed, the tribes to be terminated were supposed to be those who no longer had any need for special services. The withdrawal of these "special" services would not only save money, but would also begin the process of putting the Bureau of Indian Affairs out of a job. The implementation of the policy of withdrawal of services and trust status was based on a four-step process: withdrawal of federal trusteeship; relocation of Indians to urban centers; creation of a claims commis-sion to liquidate land claims and thereby any further reason for tribal allegiance; and the progressive dismantling of the BIA.

The Utah congressional delegation played a decisive part in this drama, providing both a liberal and a conservative approach to the pro-grammed destruction of Indian cultures. The more liberal approach was championed by Utah congresswoman Reva Beck Bosone. Her plan would have "authorized the Secretary of the Interior to survey all Indian groups under his supervision to determine when they could manage their own affairs" (Thompson 1983:7). This resolution would have provided up to twenty-five years for the termination of the tribes and of the Bureau of Indian Affairs. Bosone's plan failed to pass the Senate because of the cost of the survey and because the Senate in 1950 was not interested in a gradual end to federal supervision.

The conservative approach to termination prevailed, not as an act of Congress, but in the form of House Concurrent Resolution 108 and Public Law 280, in 1953. House Concurrent Resolution 108 was a statement of the new congressional policy of termination: as rapidly as possible, all Indians were to be subject to the same laws and entitled to the same privileges and responsibilities as other citizens, and their wardship was to be ended. Public Law 280 extended state legal jurisdiction to cover the Indians in six states and provided that the other states could also assume jurisdiction over their Indians without the Indians' consent. The perceptions of the power of a Concurrent Resolution and its legal reality are quite different; in the legal sense a concurrent resolution is "a general policy statement only and does not have even that limited effect on any future Congress" (C. Wilkinson and Briggs 1977:150–51). Nevertheless in the bureaucratic realm of policy implementation this statement would remain the underlying rationale for BIA actions for several years.

The question of where responsibility for termination lies is an intricate problem in itself (see Underdal 1977, Burt 1982). In brief a consensus developed within Congress that some form of withdrawal of BIA services was necessary. Commissioner of Indian Affairs Dillon Myer provided the impetus for an actual termination program, and Utah Senator Arthur Watkins served as the legislative strawboss. Watkins drew his attitudes toward Indians from his Mormon background and his youth, spent in the shadow of the reservation of the Uintah Ouray; his policy orientation seems to have followed directly from the Dawes Act (Thompson 1983).[1]

Dillon Myer (Drinnon 1987) had previously served as director of the War Relocation Authority (WRA), which had removed 110,000 Japanese-Americans from the West Coast to interior concentration camps. Myer became commissioner of Indian affairs in 1950, feeling "strongly that the Bureau of Indian Affairs should get out of business as quickly as possible but that the job must be done with honor" (Drinnon 1987:166). Myer replaced such IRA-oriented staff members

Table 5. The Legislative Foundation of Termination

Objective	Legal Basis
Dismantle BIA	1943 Senate Report 310
	1948 Hoover Commission
	1952 House Resolution 698
Relocate Indians to urban areas	1944 House Report 2091
Assimilate Indians	1948 Hoover Report
Transfer of BIA functions to	1951 Annual Report, secretary
local governments	of the interior
	1952 Public Law 291
An Indian Claims Commission	1928 Meriam Report

as William Zimmerman and Theodore Haas with bureaucrats that had served with him in the WRA.

Hasse (1974) relates a meeting between Watkins, Representative William Harrison of Wyoming, and Orme Lewis, assistant secretary of the interior, on February 27, 1953, in which a strategy for termination was developed. Without consulting any Indians, they decided that termination was to be a rapid process, in which services were to be transferred from the BIA to the states; tribal assets would be redistributed to individuals or tribes as groups, and trust responsibility for tribal lands would be transferred; tribal income and funds were to be disbursed on a pro rata basis; and legislation would be passed for the rehabilitation of the Indians.

While Concurrent Resolution 108 was basically a policy statement, the implementation of termination was based on a series of policy increments put forward from the very beginnings of United States Indian policy (see table 5).

Thirteen termination bills were passed between 1954 and 1962, withdrawing 3 percent of Native Americans from the federal trust relationship. The tribes affected by termination varied in their economic base and state of development, from the relatively wealthy Menominee and Klamath to the destitute Paiutes; but termination proved to be an across-the-board calamity for the tribes that it touched.

For example the termination process for the Menominee (Peroff 1982; Orfield 1983) was a slower, much better planned disaster than the ill-fated Paiute withdrawal, yet the result was no less a human tragedy. For the Klamath, with their forest lands, termination meant the loss of their land for a per capita share of the revenue generated by that sale. The money did not last, and by 1965 a BIA study revealed that the percentage of Klamath on welfare was unchanged (Orfield 1983:17).

Terminating the Helpless

As we have seen, during the mid-twentieth century, the Southern Paiutes were one of the most neglected and impoverished Indian groups in the entire United States. The poverty and powerlessness of the Utah bands, coupled with the paternalistic attitudes of their white neighbors, made them easy prey for termination, relocation, and an early settlement of their land claims.

The Southern Paiutes of Utah were not mentioned in Assistant Commissioner Zimmerman's 1947 report on Indian readiness for withdrawal (Tyler 1973:163–64) or in House Concurrent Resolution 108. Zimmerman's criteria for termination included degree of acculturation, economic resources and educational level, willingness of the tribe to be terminated, and willingness of the state to assume responsibility for services. Yet the Southern Paiutes were the first group to be considered for termination and, to some degree, served as the model for the withdrawal hearings and the implementation of termination in later tribal cases.

Responding to House Resolution 698 for information regarding the readiness of tribes to manage their own affairs, Commissioner of Indian Affairs Dillon Myer sent a questionnaire and a thirty-page memorandum (Myer 1952) to Bureau offices, with orders that BIA personnel "begin to draw up practicable plans for the termination of federal services and managerial responsibility over every tribe, band, or identifiable group of Indians in the nation" (Underdal 1977:244). These documents were to "provide a working tool in withdrawal programming" and were to be completed by September 15, 1952. Commenting on Indian involvement, Myer remarked that:

I think it may be fairly said that current congressional actions with regard to the Bureau of Indian Affairs and Indian appropriations indicate future appropriations will be limited largely to financing items which will facilitate withdrawal. This approach is already evident in both House and Senate with respect to appropriation of construction funds. Under this condition it is imperative that the Bureau develop and implement programs to assist Indians to become better qualified to manage their own affairs. Full understanding by the tribal membership should be attained in any event, and agreement with the affected Indian groups must be attained if possible. In the absence of such agreement, however, I want our differences to be clearly defined and understood by both the Indians and ourselves. We must proceed, even though Indian cooperation may be lacking in certain cases. (1952:2)

The results of this survey would prove that the Paiutes were in no condition to be cast adrift by Congress. Nevertheless political expediency dominated the discussion of their condition, eliminating any real interpretation of the evidence. The questionnaire represented the beginning of Bureau planning to terminate the Paiutes.

In response to Myer's instructions, the BIA wrote a report concerning the Paiutes, entitled "Summary Statement of Withdrawal Status." An early draft of this document, referred to as the 1952 draft, is particularly revealing in showing how ill-prepared the Paiutes were for termination. The 1952 draft states that the "Indian Peak Paiute Indians are not competent to manage their own affairs. . . . No individual in the group has ever engaged in a successful business enterprise." And yet in this same draft, when the questionnaire called for a response to "Task Remaining to Implement Termination," someone simply wrote "Complete sale of reservation and assist individuals to invest the proceeds into good viable homesites, or land within labor market areas." Thus even though the Paiutes were not ready for termination by the Bureau's own criteria, they were being pushed along toward withdrawal of services by the pressure of the incremental policy process.

The following is an excerpt from the 1952 draft concerning the Shivwits band:

Three years ago the entire reservation was leased to a single individual whose lease payments have kept the revolving credit loan currently paid. Years ago repayment cattle were issued to individual Indians. Repayments were always in arrears, and eventually stopped entirely. All of the cattle eventually disappeared, probably through illegal sale, and were finally sworn off the records. In no case have these Indians shown themselves competent to manage their own affairs without positive and direct supervision. (U.S. BIA 1952a:5)

The 1952 draft also mentions the resistance of the Shivwits to federal policy. "Refusal of Indian people to accept change of Indian customs" is listed as an obstacle to the completion of withdrawal. Under the title "Training, Relocation and Placement," the BIA solution to Indian poverty was to "relocate sufficient families to permit the Indians remaining to raise [*sic*] to the adjacent white standard of living." This policy-created "solution" is, not surprisingly, followed by a comment about the "unwillingness of the Indian people [at Shivwits] to accept permanent relocation." The Paiutes' resistance to leaving their homeland has been well documented, yet the refusal of the Paiutes to leave southern Utah was seen only as a problem or as an attitude that needed changing, not as a strong predisposition on the part of most Paiutes toward their homeland that invalidated the relocation solution.

According to the draft, the Kanosh band was also not in a position to be terminated:

Past experience in administering the affairs of the Kanosh Band indicates that, while they are the most nearly ready of our Paiute Bands, they still are not ready for Bureau withdrawal. They lack the initiative and outright incentive to actually get out and make any enterprise into a sound, paying proposition. (U.S. BIA 1952a:1)

The Koosharem band is only mentioned in outline form in the 1952 draft. This reflects the fact that they were seldom mentioned in the BIA correspondence and were seen as being under the care of the Mormon church.

Although the Paiutes were clearly not ready for withdrawal, Bureau personnel answered Myer's questionnaire with little apparent regard for the forces they were setting in motion.[2] At this point the only Paiute IRA government that could be said to function was Kanosh. The Paiutes were still relying on their traditional, slow process of internal consensus and white Mormon advisors to deal with the outside world; this political dependence left them at the mercy of the federal bureaucracy. The Northwest Shoshones and the Goshutes were originally scheduled to be terminated with the Paiutes; however, they were able to mount concerted campaigns against termination and were deleted from the legislation. The inability of the Paiutes to organize for a common purpose left them to the mercy of Senator Watkins.

The final BIA report that was sent to the commissioner was entitled "Summary Statement of Withdrawal Status." A final version of this report was published in the Federal Register, in 1953. The Summary Statement reported that no progress toward withdrawal had been made for any of the Paiute bands in the previous two years, and that no negotiations for withdrawal were then under way or completed. Only the Indian Peaks people were listed as ready for conditional withdrawal. There was no evidence provided to support even this conclusion; in fact the evidence offered by the report itself countered the assertion. Nonetheless the Summary Statement submitted to Congress indicated that none of the Paiute bands was ready for termination except for the conditional approval given to Indian Peaks. As early as June 18, 1952, the Indian Peaks band had been persuaded by the BIA to adopt a resolution to sell its reservation and to employ an attorney to pursue the sale (Emmons 1952).

It seems apparent that the reason for this approval was not that the Indian Peaks band was assimilated into the white mainstream, as indeed they were not, but that they had not lived on their reservation full-time since the early 1930s; they had lived in Cedar City, primarily with the Cedar band, in the "Indian village." Thus their land could easily be sold by the BIA and the money distributed to them on a per capita basis. According to the Summary Statement, "none of the [Indian Peaks] tribal members are experienced in business management. . . . Only one individual is considered capable of earning a reasonable income from wages." Just two of the six Indian Peaks families were considered to be "self-supporting," with their off-reservation median incomes estimated at $1500. Five of the twenty-six members could not read or write.

The Koosharem band shared similarities with the Indian Peaks band, in that almost all the members had left their small, remote reservation and were living in the city of Richfield. The Summary Statement reported that only two of nine families were self-supporting. Three Koosharem families were totally supported by welfare and four families received partial welfare support.

None of the twenty-four families at Shivwits was listed as self-supporting. Five were totally supported by welfare, and nineteen received partial support. The Summary Statement concluded that "the Shivwits have not had sufficient training and experience to successfully manage their own affairs."

Of the Kanosh group, only two of six families were considered self-supporting, with four receiving partial welfare support. Incomes from agriculture for the Kanosh Indians ranged from $200 to $1800 per year, in contrast to the farm income of whites in the Kanosh area, which was estimated at $4200. Of the twenty-seven individual Indians at Kanosh, two could not speak English and four adults could neither read nor write.

A study of the termination documents provides an opportunity to observe the changing attitude of BIA personnel in favor of termination as official Indian policy changed. The majority of Paiutes survived with assistance provided by the Mormon church, state and federal agencies, and through intermittent wage labor, the latter described in a letter from the superintendent of Uintah and Ouray, Norman Holmes (1954; original draft apparently written by Harry Gilmore), to Alexander Lesser, of the Association on American Indian Affairs as:

Section hands for the railroad, tractor operators for the government, farm hands, domestics, service station attendants, railroad section foremen, post cutters, general laborers in implement companies, poultry packing plants and sawmills. . . . The average annual income is approximately $2,268. (Holmes 1954b:2)

Holmes further noted that the Mormon church was actively engaged in helping each band toward assimilation. Virtually every BIA document dealing with the withdrawal status of the Paiutes makes reference to the activities of the Mormon church in caring for and assisting in the assimilation of the Paiutes. The assumption that the Mormons would step into the gap left by the withdrawal of federal services was apparent. BIA officials who worked in Utah generally reported with much favor on the efforts of the Mormon church and appear to have worked closely with local church leaders (this was especially true of Superintendent Gross and Parvin Church). At no time did these BIA documents really address the problems of racism, unemployment in southern Utah, or the need for education other than vocational training.

One of the various reasons given for the termination of the Paiutes was that they were receiving little federal assistance anyway. Senator Watkins observed that:

As it stands many of these Indians are in the depths of poverty, largely because they have not been able to use any of the assets in a businesslike way. They are in trust and they cannot do anything about it.

And the Indian Bureau is not very active there. It has just gone on for years and years; in the meantime, these Indians have worked a little and found out a little about their property. Some of them have leased other parts of it. No one can get paid very much because they could not get any permanent lease, or a long enough tenure to really realize much out of the property.

For that reason, it has not been of much help to them. It seems to be that it would be a great improvement in their condition to have this turned over and let them do something about it.

I think they are going to feel all right about it if we could do two or three little things which they want to have done. I do not think that they are going to hurt this wheat market if they could grow all of the wheat they are able to. (U.S. Congress 1954:49)

Watkins's observations appear to be correct in one area: the Paiutes were poor. On the other hand, the assertion by Watkins and others that the Bureau had not been helping the Paiutes is refuted by several letters

Table 6. *Paiute Income and Federal Services, Fiscal Year 1953*

Agency or Activity	Koosharem	Shivwits	Indian Peaks	Kanosh
Education & Counseling	yes	JOM* ($980)	JOM	$1800
Health	$1077	$106	$128	$408
Loan	no	$10,000	no	$10,000
Soil & Irrigation	no	$4,563	no	$12,550
Welfare	state	state	state	state
Extension	yes	limited	yes	limited
Income from leased land	none	$2000	$1010	none
Income from farming	$4,700	none	none	$1,200–$10,000

Source: Data presented in this table are from a 28 January 1954 BIA report.
*Johnson-O'Malley Act

and documents. There are scattered references to the government paying medical bills from the 1920s onward: by 1944 a Cedar City clinic billed the BIA for over $1500 in medical bills (P.E. Church 1944). In a report dated January 28, 1954, it is noted that the Indian Peaks band received limited assistance from Forestry and Grazing funds, with hospital accounts and school lunches paid under Johnson-O'Malley Act. The Bureau had also leased the 10,240 acre reservation to Anglos for the below-market figure of $1,010 per year.

For comparison, the two IRA bands, Kanosh and Shivwits, received substantial federal assistance in addition to the two $10,000 loans they had received in 1950. In fiscal 1953 the federal Soil and Irrigation Service spent $4,563 at Shivwits and $12,550 at Kanosh. From the annual reports and other available records, it appears that Kanosh received the most federal aid through the 1930s and 1940s. Sources generally tend to confirm that Kanosh was also the most prosperous of the bands (Holt fieldnotes, Earl Pickyavit interview; Palmer 1936a; J. E. White 1946a). Aside from the relative prosperity of Kanosh, the Paiutes were in such deep poverty that it must have appeared that nothing was being done for them. Nevertheless the BIA and other agencies spent over $21,612 on the Paiutes in fiscal year 1953 (see table 6). This does not include $20,000 on the books from the low-interest loans. The total assistance amounted to over $284.37 per family. In 1955 the average Paiute family income was only an estimated $375 (see chapter 4); the federal government provided a subsidy equivalent to 76 percent of the average family's income. Thus the contribution of the federal government was much greater than Watkins and others appreciated. Federal funds and tax-exempt status provided a margin of social, community, and family survival for the Paiutes. Just enough aid was appropriated to continue their dependent relationship, but never enough to break the cycle. Termination meant the withdrawal of their meager safety net and disastrous economic and social consequences for the Paiutes.

While the Koosharem and Indian Peaks Paiutes received enough aid to keep their members economically afloat, the Cedar band, living on Mormon church land, was ignored and left to the Mormons. Senator Watkins had been made aware of the problems faced by the Cedar band, in a report entitled "The Wahnquint Indians," supplied to him by William Palmer (1946a). Palmer's report gives a brief history of the Cedar band and notes that the Indian Peaks band came to live in Cedar City. Watkins (1949) wrote Palmer, saying: "I appreciate the detailed report and feel that it will give me a better understanding of their case." The Cedar band, the only band without any land of its own, was not terminated.

Exactly how and why the Paiutes came to be included on the list of tribes to be terminated remains unclear. Most scholars agree with Mary Jacobs (1974:22) when she speculates that: "Perhaps Senator Watkins, already a strong believer in the merits of termination, included these small groups from his own state both because of his own convictions and for encouragement to other legislators to terminate Indians in their own states."

The "rehabilitation" of the "Lamanites" is a critical factor in Mormon eschatology. Senator Watkins appears to have been on a holy crusade to bring the status of the Indian into line with Mormon church doctrine.

Once the bureaucratic policy machine began to move, a sort of momentum took over; tribes that did not make organized, vocal efforts to preserve their trust relationship were swept along. Paternalism played its usual role as everyone, from the local Mormons to the commissioner of Indian affairs, did what they thought was best for the Paiutes.

The Fillmore Meeting

In order to smoothe the way for termination, Senator Watkins met with members of the Paiute bands (with members of Skull Valley and Kaibab also present) at the courthouse in Fillmore, Utah, on December 30, 1953. Within eight months of this meeting, the legislation terminating the Paiutes was signed. According to a record kept by Norman Holmes, then the acting superintendent of the Uintah and Ouray Reservation, which had jurisdiction over the Paiutes:

> The Senator explained to the gathering that the purpose of the meeting was to present to them the proposed bill which would release them from government control. He further stated that it was about time to see if the Government has done a good job for the Indians and to see how many of them can take care of their own affairs. He explained that there were many people in the Indian Bureau who felt that the Indians could take over their own affairs. The Senator stated further that, under the proposed legislation, the groups listed would be given complete citizenship and that they would then be able to get all the benefits available to them from State and County governments. With the Government having control over the Indians, the State and County groups do not want to do anything for them because they feel it is a Government function since the Indians are their wards. With the Government out of the picture the State and County groups will assume their responsibility to the Indians the same as they do with non-Indians who are citizens of the state or county. (Homes 1954a:3)

Watkins then had his aide, Devere Wootton, read the proposed legislation to the meeting. Salt Lake City attorney George Morris, representing Kanosh, arrived about an hour after the meeting started and asked Watkins about taxes:

> The Senator explained the Indians would be given complete citizenship and that would mean taxes both Federal and State, however, he stated that most Indians were already paying most

of the taxes except property at this time. The next question presented by Mr. Morris was about hospitalization and education. Senator Watkins stated that all Indians would be given the same treatment that the white people received now and that would mean hospitalizations and education, through the State or County Social Workers and the Public Health Service. The Senator stated that practically all of the Indian children from the groups represented were already attending public schools. He stated that the County Clerk at Fillmore advised that if they knew the Indians were their responsibility they would budget funds to take care of them, however, so long as they were wards of the Government they would do nothing for them. (Holmes 1954a:3)

Then Superintendent Farver, of the Ft. Hall Agency, spoke "and explained that he thought the groups included in the bill would be better off under the State and County inasmuch as the Government was not doing very much for them now" (Holmes 1954a:3–4).

Arthur Johnson, a Goshute, spoke against termination and related how Indians were discriminated against and not allowed to eat in restaurants throughout the area. Senator Watkins replied:

. . . that the bill was designed to give the Indian full citizenship only and that the Indian would have to conduct himself in a respectable manner if he expected society to accept him. The Senator further stated that he had eaten in places where no one could enter unless he wore a coat and tie but that did not mean the establishment was discriminatory. Further that most restaurants have a little sign somewhere in the establishment which states that they reserve the right to refuse to serve anyone. (Holmes 1954a:4)

The manner in which Watkins glossed over Arthur Johnson's charges of discrimination by whites exemplifies the paternalism and assumption of moral superiority that was rampant in Utah. Evidence that the Utah Indians were nowhere near being able, or allowed, to assimilate into white culture was ignored by Watkins, most of the Congress, and the BIA.

In a 1982 interview, Paiute elder Clifford Jake related how he questioned Senator Watkins at this meeting:

And he [Watkins] was talking about termination among the four bands. And he was telling about it and how good it was to be free, free Indian you know. I don't think the Indians know about termination—that time some of them didn't. He came up with a lot of good things about it. Later on I—thinking about my people and they are not no educated Indians there—mostly old people, you know. I say, "Hey Senator, may I say a few words?" I told him I think my band [Indian Peaks] is not ready for termination. They don't have any livestock, any kind of income. They don't live like the white man either, we have what they call shacks—cabins. My Indian people, clear down the line clear down to Nevada. "What are they making homes out of?" he said. I told him they are making it from the white people's junk; they find a few boards, a good bed, might have a little chair, an old stool, that's where it comes from I said. That's the way they pick up their furniture. They make a house out of it. . . . Yeah, on what the white people throw away. Trash barrels! That's what they make the shack out of, I said. They had candle light and Coleman lantern. I asked him again, "Do you ever check on Indian people down toward the reservation? Do you know how they live? Did you ever visit them?" He told me "you'd better sit down, and mind your own business and shut-up." He told me that right there. I was the one that spoke up but the rest didn't. (Holt fieldnotes, July 15, 1982)

Mr. Jake was acting as speaker for the Indian Peaks band at this time and is listed by Holmes as being at the meeting, but he is not specifically mentioned in Holmes's record. Holmes's account of the meeting seems condensed and may not be a verbatim report of what actually took place. Certainly the Paiutes' perceptions of the Fillmore meeting and the report in the record seem contradictory. Clifford Jake's description of the Paiute situation, however, certainly parallels the 1952 BIA data.

Holmes spoke, suggesting that the bill would function to "release them from Government supervision and control and to ultimately give them full citizenship" (1954a:4). According to Holmes's record, the Paiutes were advised twice during the meeting that the bill was not final and that they could make changes and suggestions. Then the bill would be changed to conform with "any recommended and approved adjustments." According to Holmes's record, at no time did any of the officials mention anything but the benefits of termination, and, most importantly, at no time were the Paiutes asked if they wanted to be terminated in the first place. They were simply presented with a fait accompli.

Promises at the Newhouse

On February 10, 1954, Watkins met with representatives of the Ka-nosh Indians, including their attorney George Morris and oilman Charles H. Harrington, at the Hotel Newhouse in Salt Lake City. Harrington had acted as an advisor to Kanosh leader Joe Pickyavit and had urged that the band accept termination and grant him an oil lease on Kanosh land; he was not interested in going through the procedure for BIA approval of his oil lease. Senator Watkins prom-ised the Kanosh band that they would be exempted from restrictions on the amount of wheat they could grow and that tribal marriages would be legally recognized. These promises however, were not for-mally included in the termination legislation. When the terminated Kanosh people actually attempted, in 1957, to increase their wheat allotments they encountered a bureaucratic stone wall. When Area Director Fredrick Haverland approached BIA Assistant Commissioner E. J. Utz about their request, Utz said only that state and local boards had jurisdiction over the matter.

Dale Ashman, the county clerk of Millard County, pointed out to the Uintah and Ouray realty officer that the land at Kanosh was best suited for wheat, as it was not irrigated, and that the market condi-tions were unfavorable for other crops (Ashman 1957). Without the increase in their wheat allotment, the members of the Kanosh group simply could not make enough profit to justify their work or to meet their taxes and debts. Uintah and Ouray Superintendent Fleming was informed by Glade Allred, of the U.S. Department of Agriculture's Agricultural Stabilization Committee, that:

The 1957 wheat acreage allotment and past allotments for their land as established by the Millard ASC County Committee represents the maximum consideration that can be made under the allotment procedure. No provision is made in the allotment procedure for granting special consideration to Indians or others. (Glade Allred 1957)

This appears to have ended the matter as far as the administrators were concerned. However the unkept promise of increased wheat acreage was a major component in the failure of Indian agricultural attempts at Kanosh. The termination policy that was supposed to make the Paiutes more independent actually destroyed their last independent farming enterprise, lowered their real income, and left them more dependent on welfare than they had been prior to termination.

Congressional Hearings

Copies of the termination bill were sent to the Paiute band leaders on January 19, 1954; they were informed in letters dated February 2, 1954, that hearings on termination would be held on February 15, 1954, in Washington, D.C.:

The Indian Office in Washington, D.C. has given authority for Indian delegates selected by any of the official governing leaders of the tribes, bands and colonies affected by this bill to travel to Washington to attend hearings conducted by Committees of Congress on S.2670 on the scheduled dates provided that the particular groups concerned have ample available tribal funds to cover the expenses of such a trip. There are no federal funds available for such travel expenses nor for advances to delegates who run out of funds while in Washington. (Gilmore 1954)

The Paiutes, of course, had no travel funds; the Shivwits tribal funds balance, for example, was $149.04 as of June 30, 1951. The unusual speed of the whole process kept the Paiutes off balance; indeed, as we shall see, it was only in 1956, during the implementation of termination, that they began to realize their new and perilous position. One of the tragic ironies of termination is that the Paiutes at Kanosh were just beginning to reach an economic level where they could compete with their Anglo neighbors when termination swept away their labors. Shivwits was finally receiving some federal help, and the other bands were struggling for their social and economic dignity.

Gary Orfield (1965) has documented how Senator Watkins dominated the hearings and forced the termination of the Utah Paiutes; "only Watkins of the five Senate members was present for more than one hearing" (Orfield 1965:4). Orfield has also underscored the lack of concern for the living conditions and dependence of the tribal peoples about to be "set free":

Senate and House Indian Affairs Subcommittee Chairmen, Sen. Arthur V. Watkins, an intensely conservative Mormon religious leader from Utah, and Rep. E. Y. Berry, a South Dakota conservative, shared the beliefs that energy and initiative could only develop in the free market and the tendency to dismiss practical problems as self-serving defenses of idleness and living on welfare. They were not interested in testimony about the poverty of the tribal people and land, or witnesses pointing to problems such as the lack of resources for local infrastructure and services, absence of trained tribal administrators, and many others. These problems would not only remain after termination, but would become more damaging as federal protections and aid were withdrawn. (Orfield 1983:16)

Arguing for termination in the Senate on May 4, 1954, Watkins presented an incredible view of the degree of Paiute assimilation and a distorted knowledge of their history:

The people, numbering some 400, have been under the jurisdiction of the Indian Bureau for over half a century and due primarily to neglect by the government guardians they have been obliged to enter the communities surrounding them. Fortunately these people recognize their problem and have successfully attacked it and have fully integrated themselves into the communities around them. They have the help and assistance of the religious and civic organizations . . . (U.S. Senate 1954:5926)

At the Hotel Newhouse meeting, Kanosh representatives had also asked for permission to grant oil leases. Harrington (to whom Harry Gilmore, the superintendent of Uintah and Ouray, referred as "our enemy") wanted a lease on the Kanosh Reservation (U.S. Congress 1954:60). Senator Watkins appears to have been quite friendly to Harrington and included a letter from Harrington to Watkins as part of the *Congressional Record*, (U.S. Congress 1954:61) in which Harrington stated that "their wish is that the bill be passed as soon as possible." Gilmore (U.S. Congress 1954:62) referred to Harrington as a counselor to Joe Piccadit [*sic*] and his group. Harrington wanted to obtain an oil lease without having to follow standard BIA procedures, such as an open bidding process. Thus it was in Harrington's interest for termination to occur. Apparently referring to this meeting, Kanosh leader Mackay Pikyavit later said that "Senator Watkins said when he talked to us about termination that the taxes would be taken care of, that we would not have to be under the limitation of wheat acreage, that we could plant as much wheat as we like, but this has not been true" (Aberle 1958:2).

The testimony in favor of termination is certainly a maze of contradictions. During the course of the hearings, telegrams were received from Paiutes protesting termination. The first was from Kanosh:

We are against Federal termination bill S.2570. We desire to remain for the time being as wards of the Government, as we have lived on the reservation and have not paid taxes for so long and we feel we should live as we have always lived. Besides, what have we got to pay taxes with? We don't live like the white man, we don't even own any livestock of any kind. We owe the Government $10,000. And how do you expect us to pay taxes?

/S/ Kanosh Tribal Council
Wes Levi, Chairman; Johnson Levi, Vice-Chairman;
Lonnie Kauchoup, Secretary

The second is from the Koosharem leader, Jimmy Timikin:

Jimmy Timikin, Speaker for the Pioute [sic] Tribe, at Richfield Utah. Speaks for his people.

On May 21st 1954 Sent a Telegram to Association of American Indian Affairs, Stating We Do Not wish Termination at present time.

We have a group of about 60 members and at present have no orbination [sic]. At present time most of us can Speak English Language, but only 12 can wrote and read.

We are now fixed so part of us can go to school. We believe we better ourselves and can take better care of our people when we have better Schooling. We do not wish to separate and have to leave as it looks to us this way.

We also Believe some treaties have been Promised we do not which our Tribe to have taken from us. So we wish to have more time to learn from our people which we believe our people are Entitled to.

We do not wish Termination. Hoping to better Ourselves.

Speaker
Jimmy Timikin
Richfield, Utah

We thus have telegrams from two bands, plus solid indications that protests to termination also occurred in Shivwits (Scott 1956b) and the testimony of an Indian Peaks leader protesting termination at the Fillmore meeting with Watkins (Holt fieldnotes, Clifford Jake interview, July 15, 1982).

Unfortunately for the Paiute Nation, there was no well-organized, concerted antitermination effort. Internal bickering was more the norm. An example of their disunity was the follow-up telegram sent by Joe Pickyavit, of Kanosh, telling the committee to disregard the previous telegram sent by the Kanosh tribal council.

In hindsight it seems obvious that even those Paiutes who tacitly approved of termination were not adequately informed by the government as to the implications of withdrawal of the trust relationship. Indeed Commissioner Myer stated, in his memo of August 5,

1952, that Bureau personnel "use every opportunity to place before the Indian tribal membership the need for, and advantages to be derived from cooperative withdrawal programming effort. Tribal leaders should be encouraged to obtain maximum membership participation in this work" (Myer 1952:2).

By any standards tribal approval did not meet the parameters of informed consent. Once the decision to terminate them had been made, they were only presented with the "positive" aspects of termination. One informant said that the BIA told her that with termination "everything would be like it was before the whites came." It was not until the Bureau began to implement termination, in 1955, that they began to be informed, in a meaningful way, of the true implications of termination.

The termination legislation sped through Congress, and on September 1, 1954, President Eisenhower signed Public Law 762, the bill terminating the Paiutes after one and one-half years of BIA preparation.

Implementation of Withdrawal

The frustrations encountered by BIA personnel in their attempts to implement Public Law 762 suggest just how dependent on white advice the Paiutes really were in the early 1950s (especially when it came to legislation and tribal business ventures). In a letter to Rex Lee, Area Director Harry Stevens suggested that the (arbitrary) figure of $50,000 be allotted to prepare the four bands "to earn a livelihood, to conduct their own affairs and to assume their responsibilities as citizens." The fact that the Paiutes were in no way ready to be cast adrift is reflected in his statement that:

> The economic, social and educational levels of these people are very low. Practically all of them are full-bloods, discriminated against in their local environment and are greatly in need of special assistance and attention to fulfill the requirements of this section of the Act. They are transient workers without vocational skills. (Stevens 1954)

Table 7. *BIA Withdrawal Implementation Meetings*

Band	Meetings	Individual Contacts
Kanosh	13 meetings	"many"
Shivwits	10 regular, 5 special	65
Koosharem	8 official	"all on rolls"
Indian Peaks	5 official	8

Source: Scott (1956a)

The Paiutes were given until February 21, 1957, to prepare themselves for the end of the recognition of their special status as Indians. In order to facilitate this transition, the Bureau established a three-pronged support system, composed of: the BIA Withdrawal Office in Cedar City; an educational/vocational training program administered by the University of Utah (based on relocation); and the national BIA relocation program. Often in the background, but serving as an integral part of the termination effort, was the work of the Indian Claims Commission, which held the future promise of wealth in exchange for giving up all claims to the Paiute homeland.[3]

The BIA Withdrawal Office in Cedar City included a withdrawal director, Wesley T. Bobo, a realty officer, Frank M. Scott, and a clerk-stenographer. The office had a 1956 proposed budget of $19,965. The Cedar Withdrawal Office was not established until August 1955, and Scott did not arrive until December 1955. From the Paiute viewpoint, then, nothing had really happened since they had been scheduled for withdrawal; from the BIA viewpoint, almost an entire year of the three years allotted was lost, due to funding problems. An examination of the work and travel narratives of Bobo and Scott from November 1955 to June 1957 indicates that BIA personnel were engaged in an intensive effort to explain and discuss the implications of the termination bill with the Paiutes (see table 7).

By this time, of course, the Paiutes had been scheduled for termination, and there was nothing the bands could do but adapt to the changes being thrust upon them. From the available records and interviews, it appears that Bobo was dedicated to pursuing the exact letter of the law and bureau regulations regarding termination. Frank Scott's

Table 8. *Per Capita Value of Paiute Lands*

Reservation	Area (acres)	Enrollment	Value	Share
Shivwits	27,520	130	$70,600	$343.08
Indian Peaks	8,960	26	$36,000	$1,384.61
Kanosh	5,320	42	$86,500	$2,059.52
Koosharem	440	34	$3,100	$91.20

Source: Scott (1956b)

termination report lists the property involved, the appraised value thereof, the enrolled members of each reservation, and the individual shares (see table 8).

Scott noted that if the acreage were divided on a per-capita basis, it would not "constitute an economic farm unit." While this statement may not be strictly true in a mathematical sense, it is accurate given the quality and agricultural potential of the land. In reference to the Kanosh situation, Scott (1956b:4) revealed that "guidance and persuasion was necessary in keeping the colony site from being broken up into 42 small tracts." Scott stated that the provisions of termination were generally understood by the Paiutes; he also reported that they raised questions about relocation, taxation, medical care, and taxes. He further reported that:

It is believed that if the Indians' holdings would have been of sufficient extent and value so as to have afforded them with an economic farm unit or other means of earning a livelihood, the withdrawal of government supervision over their property would have been more satisfactory. However, the records fail to disclose any serious objection to the termination program except on the Shivwits reservation. (Scott 1956b)

The Shivwits people seem to have resisted termination and to have given the Bureau a hard time:

At the various meetings held with the Indians, considerable more interest was shown by them in what disposition was being

made of their tribal money than the benefits to be derived from
Public Law 762. They objected to the requirement of having to
pay taxes on their land. (Scott 1956b:2)

One informant (Holt fieldnotes, Reynolds interview, July 10, 1985)
recalled that: "They [the Paiutes] hated BIA, they told him [Bobo] to
get off [the Shivwits reservation]. One lady was going to hit him with
a broom."

The Bureau offered the Paiutes four options for the disposition of
their land: a tribal corporation could be established; a trusteeship for
their property could be created; the tribal property could be sold and
the proceeds could be distributed on a per-capita basis; and the property could be divided into individual parcels. It is indicative of the
poor quality of the Paiute reservation lands that no acceptable bids
were made (estimates of an acceptable bid in the case of Shivwits varied
from $1.00 to $2.56 an acre). Indian Peaks was finally sold, to the Fish
and Game Department of the State of Utah, to serve primarily as an
antelope reserve.

Scott's final report refers to the attitudes of the general public (but
not, ironically, to those of the Paiutes) regarding termination and suggested that attitudes were "about evenly divided. . . . However state
and county officials, officials of the L.D.S. Church, civil appraisers,
judges of the civil courts, and certain branches of the government were
very cooperative in connection with the termination program . . ."
(1956b:4).

BIA Area Director F. M. Haverland also submitted a report to the
commissioner of Indian affairs concerning Paiute termination, on January 3, 1957. This report (Haverland 1957) was a general analysis of the
Bureau's performance and included suggestions for future termination
projects. He stated that most of the activities of the withdrawal project
were complete by the September 1, 1956, deadline, with the exception of problems at Shivwits. In summing up the Paiute termination
experience, he observed that:

There is no question in my mind but that the continuation of
their trust relationship to the Government was not to their advantage. I do not feel, however, that the full import of the legislation

has dawned upon either the Indians or their non-Indian neighbors. I am convinced that if the adult education programs were available for at least two more years, considerable improvement in the general status of the Indian would result.

The Walker Bank Connection

In implementing the withdrawal of the federal trust responsibility, one of the duties of the Bureau was to designate a trust authority to assume responsibilities for land and Paiute minors. The convoluted logic of termination insisted that while the Paiutes were ready to be released from the federal trust relationship, another trustee had to be selected for them. First Security Bank had been approached but was not interested. The Utah state attorney general ruled that the state could not assume trusteeship (Scott 1956a). On June 20, 1956, W. T. Bobo met with William J. Fitzpatrick, vice-president and trust officer of Walker Bank and Trust, in Salt Lake City. The meeting was originally to ascertain whether Walker Bank would be interested in serving as trustee for the subsurface rights of the four Paiute bands. Bobo reported that:

> Mr. Fitzpatrick was very much interested in the trust agreement. He expressed a desire for his bank to obtain the trust, and gave every indication that a trust agreement could be worked out to their satisfaction. A nominal fee will be required. He also stated that he would like to consider including cash assets belonging to minors at Indian Peaks and Koosharem in the trust agreement. (Bobo 1956:June 18–22)

A major meeting was held on July 12, 1956, to hammer out an agreement with Fitzpatrick and his staff; also present were Assistant Area Director Harry Stevens, Agency Superintendent John Crow, and Area Solicitor William Truswell. Bobo (1956) stated that Fitzpatrick was willing "to assume the responsibilities as trustee for any properties, land, subsurface rights and moneys which we may have for transfer." Walker Bank was selected as trustee without regard for the wishes of the Paiutes; the Paiutes left the trusteeship of the BIA, but their meager resources entered the trusteeship of a bank.

Table 9. *Funds Budgeted for Walker Bank as Trustee*

Trust Agreements	$5,000
Guardianship fees	2,825
Miscellaneous costs	2,500
Total	$10,325

The tentative agreement between the BIA and Walker Bank called for charges of $500 per year (for ten years) for the trust agreements and guardianship agreements for the minors, a 5 percent sale-price fee when they negotiated the sale of lands, and a charge of 7.5 percent of any mineral royalties (U.S. Bureau of Indian Affairs 1956; see table 9).

The Shivwits band could not decide on any of the posttermination organizational alternatives put forth by the BIA (such as forming a tribal corporation or total liquidation of all tribal assets). Under pressure from the BIA, a resolution was finally passed, in July of 1957, naming Walker Bank as their trustee (Scott 1957). On August 25, 1957, members of the Shivwits council, BIA officials, and William J. Fitzpatrick, trust officer of Walker Bank, met at the bank office, in Salt Lake City. Subsequent meetings between the Paiutes and Walker Bank were both rare and short. Attorney George C. Morris was appointed by the bank to serve as attorney for the terminated bands. Apparently Walker Bank performed its required legal functions but did not expend any extra effort on behalf of the Paiutes. The BIA appraised the reservation lands that had been projected for sale in the termination plans. No satisfactory bids were received by the BIA for the Indian Peaks, Koosharem, or Shivwits reservations. The evaluations (Realty Officer 1956) were the following: Indian Peaks, $39,500; Koosharem, $2,400; and Shivwits, $57,500. There was no appraisal for Kanosh, as the land there was distributed among the residents; Walker Bank therefore performed only a minor guardianship function for the Kanosh band. As has been noted above, the Indian Peaks Reservation (surface rights only) was eventually sold to the State of Utah Fish and Game Department, for $39,500. From the proceeds of this sale, Walker Bank received $975, George Morris $250, and each of the forty-eight members (this includes the minors' estates) of the Indian Peaks band received $1,374.10/11.

Dependence and Termination

Termination under Myer was characterized by John Collier as social genocide.[4] For the Paiutes, it was a disastrous, yet unsuccessful, exercise in forced acculturation.

The Paiutes were terminated without what we know today as informed consent, and the small gains they had made under the IRA were all but wiped out. Their dependence on outside decision makers proved to be their undoing. Not only did the Paiutes lose fifteen thousand acres of land through taxes and tax-inspired sales, they also lost the ability to receive the federal services that were available to other, nonterminated Indians. And perhaps most ironically, they lost what was left of their gardens and farm enterprises, the last vestige of their ability to survive independently of outside "help."

1. Three Moapa Paiute men, 1873.
Photo by Jack Hillers. Smithsonian Institution Photo No. 1640.

2. Paiutes gambling in 1873.
Photo by Jack Hillers. Smithsonian Institution Photo No. 1624.

3. Paiute woman gathering seeds in 1873.
Photo by Jack Hillers. Smithsonian Institution Photo No. 1641.

4. A Paiute family in 1873.
Photos by Jack Hillers. Smithsonian Institution Photo No. 1597.

5. A Shivwit shelter ca. 1935. *Photo by Dr. D.E. Beck.*
Utah State Historical Society Photo No. 970.64 P.4.

6. Old housing in 1990, Cedar City, Utah, Paiute Indian Village.

7. New HUD housing in 1990, Cedar City, Utah, Paiute Indian Village.

8. Rest and recreation area, Kanosh, Utah.

9. Tribal attorney, Mary Ellen Sloan, is honored by Travis Parashont for her work on restoration and the reservation plan.

10. Paiute elder, Clifford Jake, in the 1983 Paiute restoration parade.

11. Annual Paiute restoration gathering and pow wow in 1983.

12. Pow wow grounds in Cedar City, Utah, 1991.

13. Paiute drummers in 1983 restoration parade.

14. Emily Pickyvit tans hides in Kanosh in 1982.

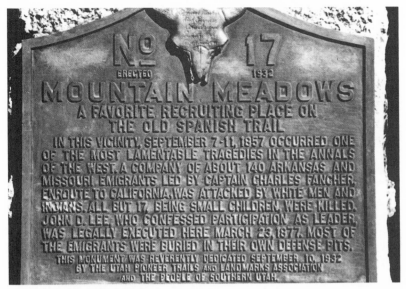

15. The Mountain Meadows monument.

16. The Paiute sewing factory in Kanosh in 1990.

17. Paiute tribal headquarters building in Cedar City, Utah, 1991.

18. Paiute tribal chair, Geneal Anderson, outside the tribal building in 1990.

19. Paiute director of education, Gary Tom, in his office in Cedar City, Utah, in 1991.

20. New HUD homes in 1990 on parcel four near Joseph, Utah.

4 THE FORGOTTEN TRIBE

THE PERIOD BETWEEN 1957 and 1975, after the federal government had washed its hands of the Paiute problem through termination, was characterized by general neglect on the part of the State of Utah for any but the most basic needs of the Paiutes. This was a time of hopelessness and social and economic decline for the majority of the Paiute people.

For the terminated tribes, the true impact and meaning of federal withdrawal of trust responsibility became increasingly clear. They suffered losses of land, federal expertise and legal protection, federal health and education funds to individuals, and training, housing, and business grants. The tribes were faced with taxes and the loss of the limited sovereignty they had enjoyed under the IRA (Wilkinson and Briggs 1977:152–54).

Congress's love affair with termination soon cooled, and as early as 1956, liberals were speaking in favor of economic development instead of termination (Prucha 1986:351). Secretary of the Interior Fred E. Seaton, in a 1958 radio speech, abandoned the policy of unilateral termination of tribes (Tyler 1973:179–80, Prucha 1986:351). During the Kennedy administration, funding was provided for tribal development projects, under the Area Redevelopment Administration (later the Economic Development Administration). The EDA administration treated tribal governments as units of local government like any other local units. Deloria and Lytle have suggested that this marks the beginning of the movement for Indian self-government (1984:196).

The years 1964–68 were presided over by Lyndon Johnson and were highlighted by the war in Indochina and the War on Poverty. Significant amounts of money were pumped into the reservations through the Office of Economic Opportunity and other antipoverty projects. In 1968 the Indian Civil Rights Act (ICRA) was passed, giving tribal courts more formal power and increasing their ability to employ legal counsel. However the ICRA also superimposed a western-style legal system, with its adversarial model. Although the ICRA repealed section seven of P.L. 280, it was not until President Richard Nixon's July 1970 message to Congress that self-determination without termination became the official policy of the government.

These events had little direct effect on the terminated Paiutes. The federal government no longer took an active interest in their affairs, and they were left in the care of the local authorities. By all accounts mortality, unemployment, and alcoholism were rampant among the Paiutes during this period. The bad economic times shattered families, and children were often raised by relatives or by whites.

The University of Utah Development Project

In the aftermath of the decision to terminate the Southern Paiutes, the BIA did make some attempts to relocate and rehabilitate its erstwhile wards. In order to facilitate the assimilation of the Paiutes into white culture, the University of Utah entered into a contract with the Bureau of Indian Affairs in July 1955. The cost of the project was not to exceed $141,996 (U.S. BIA 1955). The purpose of the contract was:

To undertake a special program of education and training designed to help the adult members of the mixed-blood group of Utes from the Uintah & Ouray Reservation, and the four bands of Paiutes residing in Southwest Utah known as the Kanosh, Koosharem, Indian Peaks, and Shivwits, to earn a livelihood, to conduct their own affairs and to assume their responsibilities as citizens without special services because of their status as Indians. Such a program may include language training, orientation in non-Indian community customs and living standards, vocational training and related subjects, transportation to the place of training or instruction, and subsistence during the course of training or instruction. (U.S. BIA 1955:1)

This university initiative was known as the Indian Rehabilitation Program and began to be implemented in November 1955, although some interviewing and reconnaissance work had been done prior to the signing of the contract. This educational-vocational training effort was headed by Y. T. Witherspoon and two field assistants who worked with the Paiutes, Leroy Condie and Henry J. Reynolds.

In his interim report, Witherspoon noted the "underdevelopment" of Paiute labor:

The relationship between the whites and the Indians is in a real sense a symbiotic one with many of the non-Indian farmers depending rather heavily upon Indian labor to get their work done, and the Indian in return gaining his complete livelihood from the farmer. A paternalistic, almost feudal system is quite apparent with at least some of the farmers being willing to furnish sub-standard housing, some sanitation facilities and a very limited sort of medical care for those Indians who return to him each year. . . . It serves to establish and maintain a relationship between employer and employee that facilitates against the employee ever gaining an independent position in society. (Witherspoon 1955:2)

Witherspoon seems to have been the first scholarly observer to note that the Paiutes had simply adapted their economy and social organization to the white presence: living in larger groups on the edge of the Mormon settlements in the winter and scattering throughout southern Utah during the spring and summer, looking for agricultural work. Witherspoon stated that the BIA relocation program had taken "out of the areas most of those individuals who might have the energy and incentive to act as leaders in the program" (1955:3). Witherspoon recognized the serious dilemma of the Paiutes at this time:

In his search for economic independence and social status in these communities the Indian moves in a vicious circle indeed. He is denied steady employment because of his subservient status and lack of vocational skills. Lacking steady employment, exploited by the whites, he does well to feed his children, let alone equip them to be self-supporting. He is not apt to marry into a position of status among the whites since the few intermarriages which do occur encounter strenuous opposition from both cultures and usually operate to diminish the status of both partners to the marriage. (Witherspoon 1955:19)

Within Witherspoon's "Interim Report" are found a number of reports from consultants. These reports were generally based on short visits with the Paiutes and interviews conducted with local whites. Among these is one by the anthropologist Elmer Smith, who stated that the work habits of the present Southern Paiute followed the basic pattern of the past; and LDS aid was a significant factor in making the Paiute content to stay in the area. He stated that in 1955, a local LDS bishop had said "that he would look after 'his' Indian laborers." The report of the economics professor Charles Larrowe reveals a picture of the Paiute living in shacks and tents without plumbing or services. He noted that the Indians contributed a pool of unskilled cheap labor that was important to the whites of Southern Utah. Commenting on whites' racial prejudice, Larrowe said that "the manager of one United States Employment Service office reflected an apparently widely-held view when he told me that the Indians are important in the southern Utah farm economy and then added, 'They're a necessary evil' " (Witherspoon 1955:17).

The report submitted by F. B. Jex dealt primarily with such attitudes and their effect on education. He stated that:

The stereotype of the Indian as "naturally" lazy, dirty, ignorant, submissive, unfit for anything but subservient labor in the white man's beet patch or corn field still appears to me to be the predominant attitude. The prevailing sentiment seems to be to help them just enough to keep them from going hungry, but not to make any difference in their lives. (Witherspoon 1955:19)

The medical consultant's report, by Dr. Glen Leymaster, listed such concerns among the Paiute as obesity, tuberculosis, an 'extreme degree' of malnutrition among young infants, and sanitation and sewage disposal problems. Tuberculosis was a continuing problem, as it was the cause of about one-third of recorded Paiute deaths between 1889 and 1926 (Spencer 1973).

This "Interim Report" is significant, because it provides one of the relatively few existing descriptions of Paiute life during the 1950s. Of particular importance is the fact that it underscored how completely unprepared the Paiutes were for termination and how their relationship of dependency upon white society was maintained. Informants and documents both suggest that help from the Mormons in the form of canned goods and bulk food items were often all that kept the Paiute above the starvation level. Yet even this help may actually have contributed to dependency, since it was only enough to "keep them alive" and still dependent on the LDS church.

> The Indian people of this general region have been assigned and in many ways seem to have accepted a subordinate and separate role in the society that is rigidly defined and deeply entrenched. At one time, they are both the objects of the paternalistic altruism of the dominant white, L.D.S. population and a ready source of inexpensive labor for white farmers, ranchers and contractors.
>
> They are treated almost universally with cordial tolerance but are practically never accepted as social equals. The Indians' own speech betrays constantly the degree to which they have accepted the whites' stereotyped image of them as being lazy, untrustworthy and incompetent for anything but the most limited of roles. (Gwilliam 1963:6–7)

Once the university program was under way, Reynolds and Condie traveled constantly between Salt Lake City and St. George, in the south. They assisted Paiutes in enrolling for classes in Salt Lake City, Ogden, and Provo for technical training as welders, body and fender repairers, and nurses' aides. General education seems to have been overlooked, in the effort to enroll the Paiutes in jobs that conformed to the stereotyped image of jobs suitable for Indians. The Paiutes in training were contacted "almost every day" by the university field team (Holt Fieldnotes, Reynolds Interview). In a 1985 interview, Henry J. Reynolds stated that: "They should never have been terminated. . . . They [the government] picked on that bunch [the Paiutes] because they thought there was no resistance . . . 'Let's start on them.' "

The reports of Leroy Condie (from December 1955 to August 1956) indicate that some Paiutes were placed in vocational training and others were provided with the first job the staff could locate. However the most pertinent importance of these reports is the delineation of numerous problems with the concept of termination itself. Condie quoted Reynolds as saying that the Paiutes "feel the government is dispossessing them of their homes."

Like so many of the policies that affected the Paiutes, the University of Utah project disrupted lives but did not last long enough to produce more than the most ephemeral results. Although a preliminary survey of the Southern Paiutes was completed in March and April of 1955, actual implementation of the program began in November 1955 and ended in August of 1956 (the contract with the University of Utah was for the fiscal year ending June 30, 1956). Of the fourteen Paiutes that I identified as participating in the Adult Vocational Training through Relocation program, not one stayed away from the reservation or finished training.

Posttermination Social and Economic Conditions

Denied federal welfare, education, health, and employment assistance (after 1957), the Paiutes found themselves plunged even deeper into poverty and despair. Increased alcohol use and early death seem to predominate in the memories of Paiute informants as they recall the posttermination days.

Several state welfare reports outlined the abysmal conditions of Paiute life during the early 1960s. The first report was written by a Washington County child-welfare worker, in 1961, and discussed conditions at Shivwits (Washington County Welfare 1961). This was a frank look at the daily life of the Paiutes as a terminated people. While the report showed middle-class biases, it also pointed out the social cost of the Paiute predicament. The report is entitled, "The November 17 Problem," and it was sent to the State Welfare Commission and Senator Wallace Bennett, of Utah. County Welfare Director C. Victor Anderson, in his cover letter, stated that:

> It is our understanding that "termination" was designed for Indian tribes which are several rungs up the ladder toward assimilation into white society. Perhaps we are mistaken on this view, which we thought was part of the philosophy of the Bureau of Indian Affairs' "termination" policy . . . We don't see how the local Paiute Indians can fit into this category . . .

Of the seven families listed in the report, four were receiving or had applied for welfare. Heavy drinking, child neglect, theft, and alcohol-related auto accidents were the norm, according to this report. Housing was substandard, and because of termination, medical services were no longer available. All of my informants stated that these conditions were an accurate representation of the posttermination condition of the Paiute (Holt fieldnotes 1981–85).

A 1962 Washington County Welfare report (Washington County Welfare 1962) indicated only negative changes in the conditions of the posttermination Paiutes. This report listed twelve families, numbering forty persons, living at Enterprise and twenty families, numbering sixty-nine people, still living at the Shivwits Reservation. My informants stated that the reason for people moving to Enterprise was seasonal work for white farmers. The patron-client relationships that had been created by the Mormon settlers seem to have changed very little.

Dependency was fostered by the common practice of daily payment for Indian labor:

> The basic idea behind this practice is that the Indian under this system can never accumulate enough money to do more than buy food for the next day. If he were paid at the end of a week's work, he would have enough money to go to one of the neighboring towns and get drunk. He would then fail to show up for work for two or three days of the following week. Thus the farmer ratio-

nalizes the low wages and the payment at the end of every day on the basis that this is actually best for the Indian since it keeps him from getting drunk and missing work. Most of the individuals in the group have never had enough money at any one time to be able to do financial planning of any importance. (Witherspoon 1955:44)

Six of the Enterprise and thirteen of the Shivwits families received public assistance and commodities. Three families at Enterprise and two at Shivwits also received intermittent help from the LDS church. The report stated that such church aid was only given in emergencies and that these families were otherwise self-supporting. Housing at Shivwits was reported as being "mostly of a hut variety": tar-papered, one-room shacks, lit by coal-oil lamps, they were overcrowded and had no flush toilets. Enterprise housing was also found to be poor. The Washington County Welfare report (1962) noted that:

> The city has a municipal housing court and has designated one row of apartments as Indian Row. These apartments are not kept in repair. Furnishings are old and inadequate; plumbing will often not be in working condition for a month before any repair is made.

Employment for the Paiutes was seasonal farm labor that lasted for about five months. Two Paiutes in Enterprise and one at Shivwits had full-time jobs paying about $1.25 per hour. Malnutrition was reported to be common, and meat was only occasionally eaten, in the form of rabbit and venison. According to the report (and also my informants) suicide, alcoholism, and child neglect appear to have been common.

In 1963 a survey of Shivwits was undertaken by Brigham Young University and conducted by Robert F. Gwilliam, Indian education counselor (see table 10). Gwilliam concluded that no changes had occurred in the relationships between the Paiutes and local non-Indians since Witherspoon's 1955 report.

These reports had indicated the continued dependence of the Paiutes on the Mormon church and their inability to participate in the economy on any level other than that of the most marginal employee.

Table 10. *1963 Paiute Survey Findings*

	Kanosh	Cedar City	Richfield
Years of Education	9.0	6.7	4.4
People per Home	5.1	7.5	4.5
Inside Toilets	33%	42%	54%
Head of Family Employed	45%	75%	54%
Welfare or Social Security	55%	25%	31%
Monthly Wages	$281	$272	$229
Percent LDS	60%	87%	91%

During the 1960s Paiutes were not even trusted to run a cash register in Cedar City (Holt fieldnotes 1982–86). With few exceptions, most notably those employed by the railroad, the Utah Paiutes remained on the periphery of the Anglo world and yet were a significant part of the system; their seasonal labor was especially important. During the early 1960s Paiute living conditions were probably at the lowest point since white occupation was completed.

Mormon Indian Programs

In the late 1940s Spencer W. Kimball, who would later become the head of the Mormon church, began to preach and write about the plight of the Indian. While individual Mormons and Mormon bishops had sporadically "helped" local Indians, Kimball's statements, and those of then-president George Albert Smith, marked the beginning of a more conscious church policy to spend more time and resources pursuing Indian converts.

William Manning (Manning n.d.) noted that, in the summer of 1949, the Paiutes he worked with as a missionary in Cedar City "knew nothing of Christianity." In 1957 Manning organized a Cedar Indian Branch, established without the permission of the church General Authorities. Other branches were established at Richfield (by Judge Reed Blomquist), Shivwits, and Kanosh. According to Manning the Kanosh Branch only lasted a "year or two," as many of the Paiutes there left the church because of an argument over a sack of flour. The original idea was to integrate the Indians into the local wards as soon as possible, but "the Indians were too backward spiritually, educationally, and socially to become active in the church program" (Manning n.d.:25). Manning suggested that "they felt too inferior to the white members to take part, and the second reason was that in several wards, they were not accepted by their white brothers and sisters, who looked upon them as a degraded, filthy, inferior people" (Manning n.d.:25).

In 1947 an Indian placement program began on an informal basis, when a Navajo girl came to live with Mormon stake president Golden Buchanan, of Sevier County. Official church sponsorship of the program followed, in July 1954 (Whittaker 1985:39). During 1971 some seven thousand "Lamanites" were sent to live in white homes; however, the number of Indians in the program declined, as the Mormon church began to stress higher enrollment standards. Thanks to the Utah congressional delegation, Mormons are able to utilize their Indian wards as tax deductions. The Mormon law firm of Wilkinson, Cragun and Barker (see next section, below) managed to get the church's placement program excluded from the provisions of the Indian Child Welfare Act (Gottlieb and Wiley 1984:166). The program has been criticized by non-Mormon authors as an attempt at cultural genocide. These critics suggest that the Mormon church is engaged in an attempt to lure the "cream of the crop" away from their traditional way of life. They further suggest that the indoctrination experienced by those on placement leaves them in a cultural limbo between both cultures, members of neither. Although some Mormon authors have questioned paternalistic and racist attitudes towards Indians (England 1985, Whittaker 1985), such attitudes have continued to set the tone of Mormon-Indian relations. A prominent Mormon author entitled his 1981 book on the Lamanites *Children of Promise* (Petersen 1981). A Paiute informant, commenting on this paternalism, stated: *"Their* Indians . . . Always taking care of them—looking after them like some livestock" (Holt fieldnotes, April 7, 1983). One Mormon bishop, referring to traditional Paiute and Native American church religious practices, stated that Christianity can only be absorbed by the Paiutes when the last vestiges of their superstition and paganism are destroyed (Holt fieldnotes, September 15, 1983). Braithwaite, in terms reminiscent of Hagan (1961), labeled the results of this continuing paternalism as hostile dependency:

In the Cedar City Paiute community the lack of mutual empathy on the general level has resulted in an intense level of hostile dependency. The Paiutes are dependent on the good graces of the Anglos for almost every facet of their lives, from the land they live on to the governmental services they must seek individually from several different agencies. In many if not most of the individual Cedar City Paiutes, hostile dependency is at a relatively advanced stage. They seem to resent those who attempt to help them the most. This in turn reinforces the condescending hostility on the part of the Anglos, and the general but hidden hostility on both sides becomes very subtle and sometimes overpowering. (1972:526)

One informant (who was in the placement program from 1965–69) expressed his feelings in this manner: "They want to suppress us . . . It makes me upset—outraged when the Mormons continue to teach in their doctrine that we're the chosen people and saying that we're from the house of Israel and then they treat us like scum" (Holt fieldnotes, Paiute informant, April 20, 1983).

The Indian placement program did, however, offer opportunities for young Paiutes to partake of white Mormon culture and stay in school longer than would have been possible without the program. A large number of the Paiute leaders of the 1980s participated in the placement program during at least part of their high school years. Despite its inherent liabilities, the program has served as an avenue for Paiutes to acquire a better education and to achieve greater economic security. Despite some cutbacks, the placement program continues into the 1990s.

As previously noted a fundamental, indeed central, premise of Mormonism is that welfare must support and promote self-sufficiency. Occasionally the Paiutes were asked to work by particular bishops at particular times, but in general they were given welfare without any work provision. As Manning (n.d.:12) said, "When I came into the branch, every Indian family was receiving Welfare aid from the Stake, whether they had an income or not . . . Some branch and mission leaders thought that it was easier to win converts by giving gifts." Thus, Mormon welfare often reinforced dependence on unearned income. The giving was, for the most part, one-way and not reciprocal. Despite the assumption of good intentions, Mormon as well as federal policy tended to reinforce a culture of dependence.

The Utah Paiutes and the Indian Claims Commission

Although there were exceptions, such as *Cherokee Nation v. Georgia* (1831), Native Americans were seldom able to appeal to the settler's courts for redress of their grievances. A U.S. Court of Claims was created in 1855, but an 1863 statute barred claims by Indian tribes based on treaties. Between 1881 and 1946, a special act of Congress was needed to bring an Indian case before the U.S. Court of Claims. This proved to be a long, expensive, and (for the Indians) frustrating experience (G. Wilkinson 1966:511–28). Prucha (1984:1018) noted that "by 1946 nearly two hundred Indian claims had been filed with the Court of Claims, but only twenty-nine received awards, most of the rest were dismissed on technicalities."

As early as 1928, the Meriam report acknowledged that tribal claims against the United Stated worked contrary to efforts to "civilize and educate the Indian" and suggested that a special commission be formed to study the existing claims. Between 1930 and 1946, numerous efforts were made to establish either a court or a commission on Indian claims.

These efforts culminated in the Indian Claims Commission (ICC) Act of August 13, 1946, creating a special commission (not a court) where tribes could settle all their outstanding grievances against the United States.[1] Only claims that had occurred before August 13, 1946, could be brought before the commission, and the act stipulated that all claims must be filed within five years, or by August 13, 1951. During this period some 617 claims were filed. Claims could be brought against the United States through the 1946 act under five broad categories:

1. Claims in law or equity under the Constitution, laws, treaties, and executive orders;

2. All other claims in law or equity, including those sounding in tort, with respect to which the claimant would have been entitled to sue in a court of the United States if the United States were subject to suit;

3. Claims resulting from treaties and contracts that were revised under duress, fraud, unconscionable consideration, or mutual or unilateral mistake;

4. Claims arising from the taking by the United States, whether as the result of a treaty of cession or otherwise, of lands owned or occupied by the claimant without the payment for such lands of compensation agreed to by the claimant;

5. Claims based upon fair and honorable dealings that are not recognized by any existing rule of law or equity. (Prucha 1984:1020)

The intent of the Indian claims legislation was to get the federal government out of the Indian business. The ICC, like termination, was an outgrowth of Congress's search for finality; the legislators wanted to settle the "Indian Question" *once and for all*; and to do that, the Indians had to have their day in court.[2] The payment of a claim would discharge all further claims against the United States concerning the matter of the suit. This would leave the United States in the morally comfortable position of having disposed through monetary compensation of all the historical wrongs claimed by the natives. Thus the ICC played an integral part in the ending of federal trust responsibility and the accompanying legal and moral obligations toward Native Americans. The commission was also seen to be a money-saving measure, as the total costs of litigation in the U.S. Court of Claims was often higher than the amount of compensation awarded (Tyler 1973:150).

There were several problems with both the ICC legislation and its implementation. Many of the commissioners were not men of great vision, and they were appointed on Justice Department recommendation. A first, and perhaps fatal, problem with the claims process was the congressional decision that Indians could only receive money and not land as compensation; many tribes in fact wanted land. From the Indian point of view, this was the major structural fault of the act, since it left no real alternatives to either taking money for compensation or getting nothing. By accepting a cash payment, the Indians legitimized the taking of their lands, and this acquiescence meant, to the whites at least, that the Indians had given up hope of ever recovering those lands.[3] Also, except in the case of Fifth Amendment takings, no interest could be charged to the federal government for the utilization of the lands after the time of taking.[4]

The second major problem with the ICC was that the Indians were to be paid compensation at the value of their land at the time of seizure, not at current land values. Compensation income, based on land values in 1850, would be inadequate to do more than provide a temporary increase in the amount of income available for investment or consumer goods.

The third issue was that the government could "offset" moneys that it had expended in the Indians' behalf and deduct these amounts from the award (J. R. White 1978:179–92). The fourth problem was that although the ICC legislation allowed for an in-house investigative division, attorneys were retained by the petitioning groups of Indians, and attorneys from the Department of Justice began preparing the defendant's (United States of America) case in a procedure reminiscent of that used in the Court of Claims.[5]

This problem was exaggerated as the Indian Claims Commission adopted many of the procedures of the Court of Claims (Vance 1969: 332–36; Rosenthal 1985:47). Hired attorneys trained in the adversarial style, proceeded as they would have in a regular court proceeding (Prucha 1984:1021), and an adversarial-court atmosphere prevailed, instead of the intent of Congress for an informal, compassionate commission. The adversarial system and the immense amounts of information presented by attorneys and expert witnesses on both sides, with their time and cost, may largely have been unnecessary had the commission relied on its own investigative division instead of on evidence presented by the opposing attorneys (Danforth 1973:370–72; Vance 1969; Rosenthal 1985:60–61). Because of the somewhat esoteric nature of the cases and because the adversarial method draws "more energy into the production of facts" (Rembar 1980:405), attorneys for both sides retained specialists, generally anthropologists and historians, to provide the expert knowledge and testimony for their positions. This associated research created an avalanche of data and publications that were instrumental in the emergence of ethnohistory as a discrete academic discipline.[6]

These problems created a fifth major flaw: the justice dispensed by the commission was justice at a snail's pace. Ten years might elapse between the hearings and the final decisions. Cases took twenty years from filing the claim to cashing the check. The commissioners that had been present at the hearings and were most familiar with the intricacies of individual cases had often left the commission by the time final decisions were written.

The Utah Paiute Claim

In October 1946 William Palmer, a Mormon church leader and amateur historian, met with Commissioner William Brophy, in Washington, D.C., to discuss the plight of the Cedar City Paiutes. Palmer was acting as a representative of the mayor of Cedar City, the Cedar City Chamber of Commerce, and the president of the Parowan Stake of the Mormon church.

The reason for Palmer's trip was that "in the last year the old agitation to drive the Indians away from the city has been renewed" (Palmer 1946b). Palmer presented Brophy with a copy of a report that he had written (Palmer 1946a) on the history and condition of the Cedar band. Brophy (Palmer 1946c) asked why the Mormon church had not built "the new homes that were part of the program when it purchased the farm land for the Indians"; and also why Cedar City "had not set up proper sanitary regulations when the Indian camp is within the city limits." Brophy informed Palmer of the impending claims commission and suggested that Palmer meet with Ernest Wilkinson, who, in cooperation with Felix Cohen, was an author of the claims act.

Wilkinson enjoyed the status of being a favorite of both the BIA and of many Washington insiders. Wilkinson's law firm became one of the major Indian claims firms, after winning a U.S. Court of Claims judgment for the Confederated Ute Bands of almost $32 million, in 1950. The Ute settlement was of precedent-setting importance and prepared the ground for the ICC. This settlement was viewed as a lavish give-away by conservative senators, who intimidated the Justice Department into a more adversarial approach. Wilkinson was later named as president of the Mormon church's Brigham Young University, in Provo, Utah (1951–71).[7]

In a letter (Palmer 1946b) addressed to "Brother" Wilkinson, Palmer mentions a meeting he had had with the Cedar band of Southern Paiutes and stated that "I told them about you and when I said that you are a Mormon and a member of the Stake Presidency there they said they would like you for their attorney." In the same letter, Palmer also mentioned a meeting he had had with the First Presidency of the Mormon church, in which "[the First Presidency] urged that the situation of these Indians and their claims for property damage and loss be pressed vigorously for an early settlement so that their unhappy situation may be relieved."

The role of the Mormon church during this period is unclear, but Robert Barker (of the Wilkinson law firm) wrote to Spencer W. Kimball, later president of the Mormon church, stating that: "It was partly because of your interest and that of other members of the Church that we undertook to represent the Southern Paiute in their claim" (Barker 1956:1).

In January of 1947, Ernest Wilkinson wrote William Palmer, requesting documentary evidence to establish that the Paiutes had exclusive possession of their lands and to create formal boundaries for the Paiute lands (Wilkinson 1947). As the case progressed, it soon became obvious that Palmer was not a trained historian or anthropologist, and some of his information was considered, at best, questionable. After 1951 Palmer played a minimal role in the claims case, until his death in March of 1960. Other expert witnesses, such as anthropologists Omer Stewart (for the Paiutes) and Julian Steward and Roberts Manners (for the Justice Department), were called into the case later. Since the 1865 Paiute Treaty had not been ratified by the Senate, any claims to land had to be predicated on exclusive immemorial possession, because joint use was not recognized in the claims act.

BIA employee P. E. Church, who served as a field aide and district agent in southern Utah, met with the Kanosh band, in March of 1951, to inform them that they must file a claim with the ICC before the August deadline. The minutes of the meeting (Kanosh Band Minutes, March 27, 1951) stated that the Paiutes were offered only one choice:

> Mr. Church informed the group that Boyden and Wilkinson, attorneys, were handling claims for other tribes and that they would handle the claims for this tribe if the tribe wanted them, which would probably be best as these people were well posted, on Indian affairs.

In June of 1951, John Boyden and Uintah and Ouray Superintendent Forrest Stone met with the Utah Paiutes at three meetings (at Kanosh, Koosharem, and Cedar City), to ask them if "they wanted to consider Mr. Boyden as their Claims Attorney" (MacDonald 1951:1). All the groups except Shivwits agreed to retain Boyden and Wilkinson. The Paiutes took the advice of the BIA, since it was identical to the advice they had received from William Palmer, and it was the only alternative offered to them by the BIA. Like Wilkinson, John Boyden was a favorite of the BIA; Superintendent Harry Gilmore had said of him that "Mr. Boyden is a man of sterling character and a very able attorney. Men of his quality are rarely identified with the interests of Indian groups" (Gilmore 1953).

Numerous lawyers were retained by the different Southern Paiute bands to represent their claims before the commission. James E. Curry entered into a contract with the Moapa band of Paiutes, in Nevada, on January 2, 1948, and assigned one-third of the case to H. Hoag and Clarence G. Linquist and another one-third interest to the Weissbrodt firm. This part of the Paiute case became known as Docket No. 88.

The Kaibab band, of Arizona, also contracted with John S. Boyden, who acted in his capacity as an associate of the firm of Wilkinson, Cragun and Barker. The Wilkinson/Boyden approach to the case was filed as Docket No. 330. Through a series of agreements between the various attorneys, dockets 88 and 330 were consolidated. The Chemehuevi (Docket No. 51) were essentially Southern Paiutes, and their claim was consolidated with that of the other Paiutes for the purposes of awarding claims money.

As the claims process began, the new policy of termination reached the stage of congressional hearings in 1954. Utah Senator Arthur Watkins, chair of the Senate Subcommittee on Indian Affairs, asked the Wilkinson firm if they would appear on behalf of the Southern Paiutes at the termination hearings. The reply was: "We had no contracts for general representation of any of the groups involved and were therefore without authority to appear" (Wilkinson, Cragun and Barker 1954). Nevertheless Glen Wilkinson did appear at the hearings, not to protect the Paiutes from termination, but to protect their claim from being nullified by the termination legislation (this action, incidently, also protected the firm's legal fee).[8]

The Justice Department, representing the federal government, attempted, in June of 1953, to work out the geographic overlap between the various tribal claims and thereby consolidate the Southern Paiute case with the California, Ute, and Klamath dockets. In December 1956 the Justice Department also tried to consolidate the Paiute claims with the Navajo and Hopi claims. These tactics were successfully confronted by the Southern Paiutes' lawyers, with some loss of jointly used land. The government lawyers were attempting to weaken the individual tribal cases through consolidation and to remove lands from the settlement that had traditionally been jointly utilized by two or more groups.

This points up the real problem of land tenure based on "exclusive use and occupancy," which is essentially a western legal concept; it was, in general, totally inappropriate to the Native American system of land use (Albers and Kay 1985). Native Americans often utilized the same lands at different times of the year, or else their boundaries were vague and overlapping. Exclusive occupancy was also supposed to be from "time immemorial," suggesting that Native American groups had been static, sedentary communities for thousands of years.

With the Tee-Hit-Ton case before the Court of Claims, in 1944, government attorneys successfully challenged the right of Indians to land claims based on original Indian title (Cohen 1982:443). However the legislative history of the ICC Act clearly demonstrates that the intent of Congress was to allow Indian groups to base claims on original title. The claims legislation (H.R. 4497) stated that the commission should hear "all claims of every nature whatsoever."[9]

Internal memos and letters between Ernest Wilkinson and Carl

Hawkins indicate that the Paiute claim was rated a fifth priority by the Wilkinson firm; this was the lowest priority given by the firm to Indian claims cases. In 1955 they were engaged in thirty-nine Indian land-claims cases and had eight tribes as general clients. A letter from Ernest Wilkinson to Carl Hawkins indicates that Wilkinson had loaned the firm $116,000, and that they were having a cash-flow crisis (they anticipated an income of $60,200 and expenses of $77,770); therefore, it was certainly in the Wilkinson firm's best interest to settle the Paiute and other claims cases rapidly. For law firms engaged in cases contingent on success, however, cash-flow problems tend to be the norm and not the exception.

One of the methods available for accelerating the process was through a compromise approved by the particular Indian group. This approach, however, allowed for no appeal from the Indians to either the U.S. Court of Claims or to the Supreme Court, as did the normal land claims process. A compromise was formulated by attorneys representing the Southern Paiutes and Chemehuevi, summarized as follows:

> The settlement negotiations themselves were carried on, on behalf of the Southern Paiute and Chemehuevi jointly, by Mr. Cragun, Mr. Lazarus and Mrs. Horn, sometimes joined by Mr. Abe Weissbrodt. Numerous office and inter-office conferences were held among the attorneys representing the petitioners, and the negotiations themselves were spread over a period of several months. Not only did we have to determine what would be a fair settlement for the Southern Paiute and Chemehuevi that would be acceptable to the defendant, we had also to determine what would be a fair share of the settlement figure for the Southern Paiute as against the Chemehuevi. A division based upon the areas claimed and conceded by each in ratio to the total joint claim was agreed upon between attorneys in Docket Nos. 88 and 330 and attorneys in Docket No. 351. (Weissbrodt and Boyden 1965:30)

The precise value of the Paiute land was never determined, since the compromise executed on behalf of the Paiute and Chemehuevi consisted of $8.25 million for 29,935,000 acres of land; the Paiutes were to be paid 27.5 cents an acre for their land. The attorneys made only one reference to the method they used to determine how much money they wanted for the Paiutes:

> Mrs. Horn collected information on the soils and minerals of the subject area, calculated roughly the acreage and the number of people involved, and brought together data relative to values set by the Commission or otherwise obtained of similar type lands. Subsequently, during the course of the negotiations, she studied GAO records to determine (1) probable amount of offsets chargeable against a Southern Paiute award, and (2) probable value of the accounting claim asserted in Docket No. 330-A. She also reviewed the record in the case for data on which to base a date of taking. (Weissbrodt and Boyden 1965:28)

The Wilkinson firm was advised informally by the ICC that the compromise was fair and would probably "be accepted if first approved by the Indians and [the Department of the Interior]" (Cragun 1964:3).

On July 6, 1964, the attorneys for the Paiutes submitted a compromise solution for the settlement of the Paiute claim to the attorney general; on October 9, 1964, the attorney general accepted the offer (Indian Claims Commission Proposed Findings of Fact 1965:19). The most critical part of the compromise was apparently an agreement between the attorneys on both sides that no offsets would be made by the government if the Paiute attorneys set a reasonable price on the land. Yet in the case of the Paiutes, the major offsets the government could have held against them were two $10,000 loans (part of which had been repaid by white rancher's grazing fees) and the expenses incurred by various water and irrigation projects. Nevertheless according to John Cragun, the United States claimed $600,000 in offsets against the Southern Paiutes (Cragun 1964:2).

Cragun suggested that a compromise would eliminate "risks, expenses and delays" associated with "original title claims and issues of value, offsets and appeals" (Cragun 1964:3). He admitted that the government's claimed offsets would be considerably reduced if the claim were prosecuted instead of settled. He did state, however, that the

Paiutes would be compensated for less acreage than they had claimed. These offsets, then, would have been minimal in comparison to the settlement amount or the lawyers' fees.

The BIA and the Paiute lawyers held a series of seven meetings with the bands between December 5 and December 9, 1964, in which the terms of the compromise settlement were explained to them by three of the attorneys (Gormley, Boyden, and Horn). At the conclusion of these hasty meetings, which lasted only a few hours, the Paiutes were called upon to approve the compromise. The compromise was presented to the Paiutes with the condition that it would take a majority of all those voting to reject it. Thus if one band rejected it, that band could not veto the whole claims settlement (Shapard 1964).

In the Cedar City meeting, John Boyden told the Paiutes that the attorneys "feel that this is a good settlement and will be in your best interest." Boyden listed five reasons they should settle: the settlement might not be as large if it were taken through court; it would take five to seven additional years; about one million dollars in interest would be lost in that length of time; it would be expensive to continue the case; and neither a larger settlement nor an equivalent amount could be expected if the case were continued (Shapard 1964:1).

In the meeting at Moccasin, Arizona, Gormley told the Paiutes that if they refused the compromise, just the evaluation stage of further litigation would cost $100,000 and take five to seven years. He did say, however, that, in his opinion, further litigation might recover 13 million acres! How this would be possible, given the rules of the Indian Claims Commission, was not explained. This is the only statement recorded in the seven sets of BIA minutes that even remotely suggested an alternative to the compromise (Shapard 1964:2).[10]

The subject of termination came up at each meeting, and the Paiutes were told that the claims money had nothing to do with termination. They were also informed that if they tried to fight the compromise, they would get less, not more money. Burt (1982:81) suggested that, in some cases, the BIA used a carrot-and-stick approach in telling tribes they had to go along with termination or their claims money would not be forthcoming. There is no explicit mention of this with the Paiutes, but some of the sources hint that such pressures were perceived by various Paiute leaders.

When the question of how to distribute and/or allocate the funds came up, the Utah Paiutes were told by their attorneys: "Let's decide if you want the money first. Then put pressure on your man in Congress" (Shapard 1964:Las Vegas minutes, 4).

At each of the meetings, the Paiutes voted to accept the compromise settlement and then voted to pass a resolution calling for a full 10 percent fee and repayment of expenses for the attorneys. When asked what the usual attorney fee was, the reply was "it depends on the case; it can be 25–40%" (Shapard 1964:Moapa meeting, 3–4). Presented in this manner, a 10 percent fee must have sounded like a bargain.

At the Richfield meeting, the majority of questions were asked by the non-Indians present (the only identified non-Indian was Roy Chidister, a Mormon church worker). The local Mormon bishop and a councilman were present at the St. George meeting. The total vote was 220 in favor and 0 opposed.

Chief Commissioner Watkins apparently wanted the Paiute case settled before the end of 1964, but because of the Christmas holidays this was not possible (Gormley 1965). Twelve Southern Paiutes testified before the ICC, on December 17, 1964, and on January 18, 1965, the Southern Paiutes were awarded the sum of $7,253,165.19 for 26.4 million acres of land, or 27.3 cents per acre. The per-capita share of the funds awarded the Southern Paiutes amounted to $7,522. The findings of fact were rewritten at least three times (once with input from the chief commissioner; Cragun 1965).

The contract attorneys filed a petition to the ICC for a full 10 percent fee. The ICC granted them a 9 percent fee plus expenses. The fact that the attorneys were not granted the full 10 percent fee may indicate that the ICC felt that the early compromise settlement benefited the lawyers.[11] The attorneys were paid a fee of $652,784.86 and, later, $44,855.61 in expenses. By March 21, 1968, the accrued interest on the Paiute accounts was $697,640.47. This more than made up for the attorney fees and the $21,601 expenses of the BIA enrollment planning effort.

Waiting for the Jubilee

Once the Paiutes had won their case, the problem then became one of how to administer and distribute the award. In a report on a trip made to the Southern Paiute communities in April of 1965, Paul Brill summed up the Southern Paiute attitude:

> It is fairly obvious that a total and complete per capita distribution of the judgment funds is what the Southern Paiute Indians really want. However, these people are fully aware of the situation of the four terminated bands in Utah and will probably accede to some form of programming along with a partial payment rather than hold out for a total per capita and risk the possibility of accompanying terminal legislation. (Brill 1965)

Several individuals and groups, including the governor of Utah, went on record against per-capita payments. BIA Area Director Leonard Hill noted that: "The basis of the concern is the fact that these people generally are impoverished, uneducated, unemployed, and inexperienced in handling money of amounts expected to be disbursed from the claim" (Hill 1968:2).

In a band meeting held April 3, 1967, the Cedar band unanimously accepted a spending plan for their claims money. It was decided to distribute the money in equal proportions to those who were eligible, with the following restrictions:

1. Each individual must first pay all his personal bills;
2. Adults' money would be used to bring family housing up to desirable standards;
3. Children's money would be put into a bank and restricted to educational or homebuilding uses;
4. Any additional money would be used to develop programs such as travel- and tourist-oriented businesses. (Cedar Band Meeting Notes 1967)

While this spending plan reflected the best intentions of both the council and the tribal members, it was in no way legally binding.

Table 11. *Sources of Paiute Income*

Income Source	Percentage of Total
Seasonal farm and ranch work	45%
Railroad maintenance	17%
Industrial/commercial work	17%
Maids, dishwashers, odd jobs	21%
Government jobs	3%

Neither the State of Utah nor the BIA wanted to accept responsibility for oversight of the claims funds; this was especially true in the case of the four terminated bands. After a series of proposals by the attorneys and state and BIA officials, the administration of the claims money became the responsibility of a finance trust committee elected by each band. John Boyden played a major role in these negotiations, as the attorney of record for Docket No. 330 and as the chair of the Utah Governor's State Board of Indian Affairs. Each trust committee was composed of three Paiutes and three whites from the local community.

Despite numerous suggestions to the contrary, no funds were set aside for collective ventures by the Utah Paiutes; all were allocated on a per-capita basis. The major role of the trust committee was to safeguard the minors' money and provide for their health and educational needs until they reached their age of majority. This formula was apparently decided by the State Board of Indian Affairs, prior to notifying the Southern Paiutes (Utah State Board of Indian Affairs 1970). Again Paiutes were brought in to participate only after the key decisions had been made by the paternalistic attorneys and state officials.

Funds to pay the judgment were appropriated on April 30, 1965, and Senate Bill 3229 was introduced on March 26, 1968, to authorize distribution of the award. Until the award was actually made, the money was placed in several interest-bearing accounts. In order to implement the claims award and to establish who was actually a Southern Paiute, the BIA conducted a social and economic survey in 1968, which serves as one of the few indicators of the lack of progress made by the Paiutes after termination (Hill 1968). This survey established an official membership roll for the Paiute bands and gathered background information in order to evaluate claims money distribution plans (see table 11).

According to the survey conducted by Leonard Hill (1968), 73 percent of income came from wages and salaries, while 20 percent came from welfare and 7 percent from Social Security, railroad retirement, and rental allowances. The figure of 45 percent seasonal farm and ranch work suggests that when these seasonal jobs did not exist, those Paiutes involved in it were dependent on some form of welfare. The average income per family from all sources was $2,746, which amounts to a per-capita income of about $612. Hill's account seems to agree with a report concerning the Cedar City Paiutes written in 1968 by Enrollment Officer Norman Holmes.

Holmes's report centered on employed Paiutes that worked for the Union Pacific Railroad as section hands for about $5000 per year. He cited seven Paiutes as then employed by the Union Pacific and one retired. He also mentioned two Paiutes who worked for the Coleman Company, earning about $375 per month (Holmes 1968).

The claims award was finally distributed in 1971 (see table 12).

Leonard Hill (Hill 1968:15–16) claimed that housing was the first priority among the Paiutes for their expected claims money. Housing was followed by payment of debts, living expenses, and investments. Other preferred uses of the claims money according to Hill, included education, purchasing small businesses or cattle, and medical and dental services. Funds from the claims award were in fact utilized by the Paiutes for housing, the purchase of trucks and automobiles, and the payment of debts. (Holt fieldnotes, Paiute informant #19, February 13, 1983). Their experience with these per-capita payments parallels that of the Klamath (Orfield 1983:17). The Klamath received $43,000 each, in 1961, for tribal assets; by 1965, one-fourth had less than $5,000 left. For the Paiutes the land claims money that was supposed to facilitate their entry into the white world was soon gone, and they were left with nothing: no land, no money, no trust relationship, and no expectations for a brighter future.

Although the Indian Claims Commission, like relocation, was a part of the overall termination package, its effects and the actual payments made to the Paiutes took place well after the termination period. Four-

Table 12. *Southern Paiute Claim Awards*

Band	Adults	Minors	Total	Award
Cedar City	35	57	92	$692,068.23
Indian Peaks	18	9	27	$203,106.96
Kanosh	30	28	58	$436,303.84
Koosharem	24	22	46	$346,034.08
Shivwits	87	77	164	$1,233,686.72
Totals	194	193	387	$2,911,199.83

Source: U.S. Bureau of Indian Affairs 1971

teen years passed between the time termination was finalized and the time the money was distributed. The promise of payment for lost land appeared early in the 1950s, but the tortuous legal process took so long that the actual payments took place twenty years later. Thus the Indian claims process was, for the Paiutes, a bewildering twenty-year wait. From the Paiutes' perspective, the length of the claims process negated most of the potential good that could have come from having a per-capita payment during the early 1960s (Holt 1987:112–38).

The efforts of the Indian Claims Commission did not entirely come to naught, however. The money helped to provide housing for the Indian Peaks band, either new or remodeled homes for others, and educational options for some younger people. One of the many effects of the claims case was to increase Paiute political activity and awareness. After ten years of organizational inactivity, their leaders began to learn (and in some cases relearn) the skills necessary to deal with the federal government and to administer a tribal government.[12] In many ways the claims case laid the groundwork for the 1980 restoration of tribal status to the Paiutes (Holt 1987:139–68). But in the end, the Paiutes had renounced, at least in the eyes of the federal government, their rights to over twenty-nine million acres; they had gained only a small, temporary, monetary advantage.

Nationwide the major benefactors of the Indian claims process were several large law firms. The largest of these (by number of claims cases) was Wilkinson, Cragun and Barker. Along with John Boyden, the

Wilkinson firm was presented to the Paiutes by both the Bureau of Indian Affairs and Mormon officials as a source of specialized knowledge and expert advice; but the attorneys stood to make millions from the various land-claims cases. They also, of course, did run some risk in accepting long-term cases on a contingent-fee basis. Their expert advice, however, was often simply informing the Paiutes of their "best" option. Neither Ernest Wilkinson nor John Boyden were villains, as has sometimes been intimated.[13] Nevertheless, they were both men of their times, were immersed in Mormon ideology, and persuaded that they knew what was best for the American Indian.

5 RESTORATION
and
RESERVATION

FROM 1970 UNTIL the present (1991), federal policy toward Native Americans has been characterized by the phrases "Indian self-determination" and "government-to-government relations." The ideas of termination and total assimilation faded from the official policy agenda, but still refused to die. Termination-assimilation remains an unspoken model for the ultimate fate of the American Indian among many policy makers.

During the 1960s and 1970s an influx of federal money into the reservations created a period of revitalization and reorganization in Indian country. This was a time when Native Americans might realistically accomplish modest goals and improve their social and economic positions. Programs and economic growth were, however, not easily available to the terminated tribes. Their share of the optimism of the 1970s was tentative compared to that of their nonterminated cousins. An added complication was the abiding paternalism of earlier eras, which still existed as tribal governments continued to draw upon federal resources and attempted to adapt monies and programs to local needs. Since the federal government continued to control the flow of money into the reservations, it thereby controlled the rate and direction of development.

The poverty and misery associated with termination forced Congress, at least temporarily, to reconsider its preferred policy and to restore federal recognition to terminated tribes in the 1970s. Nevertheless, restoration of trust status to the terminated tribes proved to be a long and perilous journey that is still in progress.

The Trail Toward Restoration

The first suggestion that the Paiutes would attempt to restore their relationship with the federal government came in 1958, less than a year after they were officially terminated. While working on the Commission on the Rights, Liberties, and Responsibilities of the American Indian, Sophie Aberle met with a group of Paiutes in Cedar City on June 4 and 5, 1958. Aberle's fieldnotes (Aberle 1958) mention that there was a general agreement at this meeting that the Paiutes were worse off after termination than before (see also Brophy and Aberle 1966:193–96). The fieldnotes contain the following:

> Bishop Manning said that the white people he knew did not understand what was going on when the termination bill was being discussed. The issues meant little to them. The non-Indian people, if they thought about it at all, believed it would be a good idea if the Indians could take their place in shops, garages, etc. Now, he said, the white people are no longer indifferent. After this statement, the Indians spoke among themselves about getting up a petition asking to be taken back under BIA. Mr. Manning said he thought that the non-Indians in Cedar City would be glad to sign such a petition with the Indians. (Aberle 1958:3)

It took the BIA until 1965 to realize that the Indian Peaks and Cedar bands were two different entities (Butler 1965; Graham Holmes 1965). Five years later, in August of 1970, the BIA informed the Cedar band that they had never been terminated and were eligible for federal services. By 1972 Acting Assistant Area Director Charles Worthman stated that:

> The status of the Cedar City group was last considered at the time the vote was being taken on the proposed Southern Paiute compromise settlement of the claims filed with the Indian Claims Commission. At a meeting held in Cedar City to consider the settlement, two chairmen were selected, one for the Cedar City group and another for the Indian Peaks group. . . . The individual Paiutes living at Cedar City have not been terminated; however,

the land they occupy is not a recognized Indian reservation, and they would be treated as any other group of American Indians who do not have a Federally recognized Indian Reservation.

The possibility of their participating in programs designed for Reservation Indians is remote. In order for us to recognize them at this point as a separate group of Indians for the purpose of participating in Federal Indian programs, it would be necessary that Congress enact special legislation. (Worthman 1972)

Although the Indian Peaks and Cedar bands lived in similar circumstances and often in the same "Indian Village" in Cedar City, the fact that one group could now receive services and the other could not was perceived as a gross injustice. These perceptions provided the impetus for an Indian Peaks leader, Clifford Jake, to begin investigating how they could reverse their terminated status (Braithwaite 1972:407–9). Even the usually quiet Koosharem band in Richfield became more vocal over their need for land:

. . . We are asking you to give us some of our ancestral lands back.

We lost our land a little at a time through treaties, by people fencing us out, by the government just taking it. Today we have no land, no place to camp except on land that people say is theirs and not ours. We do not own the houses we live in, the land we live on, or no water to even raise a garden with.

We have received no money from the government or anyone else for the loss of our land. A lot of our children have been taken away by welfare and we see them no more. Our mothers have cried many tears for their children are gone. Even if we received money from the government, maybe we couldn't get our children back.

Most of us drink too much but maybe you would too if you were one of us. Please do not judge us too harshly for our lives are not easy.

When we walk downtown we are looking for help. We do not like to beg, but we have so little to live on. Every little bit counts. We are strangers in our own land.

We are grateful for what help we have been given, but soon we will all be gone unless something different happens to us. We want to live like everyone else and see our children healthy and happy. In the name of SHINAALV, the name we use when we pray to our God, please help us.

Please give us some of our land back, enough to dignify our lives. (Woodrow Pete et al. 1968)

In 1971 Mackay Pickyavit of Kanosh, who was a member of the Utah State Board of Indian Affairs, discussed the question of regaining federal recognition with Bruce Parry, who was then director of the Utah State Division of Indian Affairs. They decided to await the outcome of the Menominee Restoration Bill, which was then under consideration by Congress, in the hopes that it would provide a useful precedent for Paiute restoration.

The Early Organizing Efforts

The beginnings of an all-band, incremental effort to organize new institutions and to provide for economic and social development began as Paiute disenchantment with their situation merged with white efforts to assist and guide them to a better state. The first new institution was the Cedar City Indian Community Development Council, which was initiated by the white community and organized through the efforts of staff members of Southern Utah State College. The council was incorporated on August 13, 1970, in order to apply for federal funds (Braithwaite 1972: 415–19). This organization was to represent all Native Americans in Cedar City and represented the first organizing effort outside the Mormon church proper since the educational efforts associated with termination. Perhaps because it was a white-initiated council the CCICDC never accomplished much and was short-lived.

During this same period (1970–73), VISTA volunteers also worked with the Paiutes. Their major contribution appears to have been to reinforce the idea of the Paiutes organizing themselves and looking beyond the LDS church for assistance (Spencer 1973:28). Nevertheless the CCICDC, VISTA, and the Paiute land-claims settlement money (which began to be distributed in 1971) provided both a historical foundation and concrete practice for the Paiutes' organizational skills. Commenting on the attitudes of the Anglo community toward the Paiutes, Braithwaite stated that:

> In Cedar City, although the Anglos started from the same paternalistic attitude base the behavior of the general Anglo population in Cedar City has evolved into a remote, impersonal, and threatening relationship for the Paiutes. Instead of empathy on the part of the Anglos, their general attitude can best be called one of "condescending hostility." (1972:525)

A new organization that proved to be the springboard for federal recognition was the Utah Paiute Tribal Corporation, constituted in 1971 and incorporated in July 1972. The U.P.T.C. Board of Directors was comprised of five elected band representatives, with a chair elected from the five, and then a sixth member being elected to fill the vacancy created by the election of a chair. The Paiute Tribal Corporation began to function as a de facto tribal government. A Paiute Housing Authority was eventually formed, in February of 1974 (Utah State Board of Indian Affairs 1974) and forty-two HUD housing units were built between 1976 and 1981. In March of 1974, the Utah Paiute Tribal Corporation received a $22,500 grant from the Four Corners Regional Commission to locate businesses to occupy the three multipurpose industrial buildings that were nearing completion and to provide for the employment of tribal members.

Efforts toward restoration of tribal status resumed on September 13, 1973, when petitions were circulated among the bands calling for the restoration of federal recognition. The Utah State Director of Indian Affairs, Bruce Parry, contacted BIA Area Director John Artichoker and then met with Morris Thompson, Commissioner of Indian Affairs, in Phoenix, Arizona. Both were supportive of restoration efforts, and a report was drafted by Mary Ellen Sloan, a law student working for the Regional Solicitor's Office. This nine-page memo established that the Paiutes had never met the criteria established for termination and that promises were made by Senator Watkins but were not kept. The report also provided a policy statement on the errors and evils of termination.

Congress enacted the Menominee Restoration Act on December 22,

1973, and on April 22, 1975 Menominee land was restored to trust status (Prucha 1986:372). The Menominee and Siletz restorations gave the Paiutes a model for both the legislation and the process of regaining trust status.

In 1975 an Indian attorney named Larry Echohawk was approached by a member of the Paiute Tribal Corporation Board and by Bruce Parry to initiate the legal process required for restoration.[1] It was determined by Echohawk and those involved in the restoration effort that the normal court process would not be effective and that legislation would be necessary to restore the federal trust relationship (Holt fieldnotes, Sloan interview, July 30, 1985 and Echohawk interview, August 19, 1983).

The year 1975 was marked by a series of meetings between the Paiutes, their white advocates, and the BIA. On January 31, 1975, a meeting was held in Cedar City, attended by approximately 125 people. The possibility of reversing termination was discussed, and Clifford Jake, spokesperson for the Indian Peaks band, stated that his band "was in favor of seeking restoration for itself" (Mehojah 1975). The band representatives decided to schedule further restoration meetings.

Between March 6 and 8, 1975, a series of meetings sponsored by the Utah Division of Indian Affairs and the BIA were held in Richfield with the Kanosh and Koosharem bands; in Cedar City with the Indian Peaks and Cedar bands; and in St. George with the Shivwits band. At these meetings various forms of tribal government and the advantages and disadvantages of restoration were discussed (Mehojah 1975). The meeting at Richfield is of special interest, because of a statement made by Richfield's mayor, Kendrick Harwood, that he "was against termination at that time, and fought it, but nothing could be done to forestall the Government from writing the Bands off." According to Mehojah's record, Harwood further stated that "the minutes of the county commissioners will show they were against the termination action of the Government." Harwood was serving as chairman of the County Commission when the bands were terminated.

In his report on the Richfield meeting, Dee Wilcox, a BIA social worker who was destined to head the future Southern Paiute Field Station, in Cedar City, reported that "it is obvious that there has never been any concerted effort on the part of the community to assist the Paiute people" (Wilcox 1975).

According to a memo written to the band chairmen on March 12 (apparently developed from the early March meetings), the advantages and disadvantages of reinstatement as perceived by Bruce Parry were as follows:

Advantages:

1. Protection of reservation land base.

2. Relief from taxation.

3. Federal programs, such as: housing, education, grants and loans, welfare and medical benefits, water and sewer development, government revenue sharing, agricultural extension services, business development grants, and contracts with the BIA to provide own programs.

4. Certain attributes of sovereignty.

5. BIA and Indian Health Service employment preference.

6. Technical assistance from BIA.

7. Investment services for tribal funds.

Disadvantages:

1. Secretary of Interior must approve many tribal decisions.

a. Control over tribal money.

b. Approval of contracts.

c. Approval of tribal attorney and his fees.

2. Restrictive laws that narrow tribal operations.

3. Red Tape! (Parry 1975)

The records of these three meetings make it obvious that the Paiutes were overwhelmingly in favor of reinstatement of federal status. State Indian Affairs Director Bruce Parry indicated to the State Indian affairs board that only three Paiute adults were opposed to reinstatement; all others were in favor (Utah State Board of Indian Affairs 1975).

Utah Senator Frank Moss requested that the BIA draft proposed legislation. Senator Moss and Utah Congressman Gunn McKay, both Democrats, were ready to introduce and support the legislation when Moss was defeated for reelection, in 1976.

The original draft of the restoration bill provided for each Paiute band to be restored as a separate political entity, which was essentially the pretermination status quo. A BIA memo (Ducheneaux 1975) of July 2, 1975, discussed a redraft of the bill that included one major change: that the Paiutes be restored as a single tribal unit. This position represented the existing de facto situation under the Utah Paiute Tribal Corporation. The memo noted that giving the Indian Peaks band semisovereign status when its membership was only twenty-seven people was "stretching the concept of sovereignty." It also noted that these small bands, acting alone, would lack an adequate land base, income, and leadership to operate an effective government. Secondly the memo noted that "it is economically infeasible for the Bureau to provide services and programs to five widely separated bands." The report concluded that the bands shared cultural ties and that a single tribal government would be in a better position to compete against larger tribes for money. In April of 1976, a third draft of restoration legislation was prepared, which proposed to include all the bands under one tribal government.

After the defeat of Utah's Democratic Senator Moss by the Republican Orrin Hatch, the Paiutes had to establish a new relationship with Hatch and the Republican congressional delegation. Although Senator Hatch was the first to be persuaded of the necessity of restoring the Paiutes, he remained a lukewarm advocate. Congressman Dan Marriott became the House cosponsor and remained the Paiutes' staunchest ally within the Utah delegation. The process of winning over the delegation essentially took two years.

The Final Push

In 1978 Mary Ellen Sloan was approached by Larry Echohawk to write legislation to create a federally recognized tribal entity for the Paiutes. By April 1978 legislation similar to the Siletz Restoration Bill, which had recently been passed by Congress and which provided for a reservation plan to be presented to it, was submitted by Sloan to the staff of the Utah congressional delegation. This draft included provisions to establish a single tribal government, with a format similar to the Utah Paiute Tribal Corporation, and to require the secretary of the interior to undertake a study of a plan for a Paiute reservation. After drafting this bill, Sloan joined the Echohawk law firm, in May of 1978, and became the lead attorney for the Paiute restoration effort. The plan was presented to Senator Hatch at a meeting in his office.

In July of 1979, the first meeting of the Paiute Restoration Committee was held. This group was formed in order to lobby for the best possible legislation for the Paiute cause. The committee was composed of the Paiute Tribal Council and influential Utahns from diverse backgrounds. Tactics included encouraging individuals with contacts to write letters of support, make phone calls, and to encourage latent Mormon support and sympathy for the Paiutes. Historical and other materials were compiled to support the Paiute claims that they had suffered unjustly as a result of termination. The essential strategy devised by Sloan and the committee was one of legislative advocacy.

This approach was utilized and refined throughout the restoration phase and was applied, with some brilliance, during the reservation phase, which followed restoration. The strategy was basically a search for support (mostly in the form of letters) from influential third parties. Sloan also received suggestions and guidance concerning materials to be presented to the legislative committees from Charles Wilkinson, who, at that time, was at the University of Oregon, Eugene. There was little interest in nor was there serious opposition to the restoration from the white population in southern Utah. But there was opposition to the idea of inclusion of a reservation plan from conservative circles.

In June 1979 Senator Hatch introduced legislation designed to restore federal status to the Paiutes of Utah. This draft deleted Section 7 from Sloan's draft, however, which would have required the secretary of the interior to undertake a study and develop a plan for a reservation. The House version of the bill was sponsored by Congressman Dan Marriott; Section 7 of the House version also did not allow for new lands to be added to the Paiute land base.

On August 29, 1979, Senator Hatch held a meeting at Southern Utah State College, in Cedar City, to assess opinion on Paiute recognition (Ragsdale 1979). At this meeting several Paiutes (forty to fifty were in attendance) spoke strongly in favor of restoration, the need for a land base for their people, and of discrimination by local whites. Several examples of blatant discrimination against Paiutes were cited. This testimony seems to have convinced Hatch that the Paiutes were in need of his help. The president of Southern Utah State College noted that the Paiutes, because of their terminated status, were unable to attend college, whereas Indian students from recognized tribes were eligible for tuition and other assistance. Speakers also included county commissioners of Duchesne and Uintah counties (invited by Hatch), where the Uintah and Ouray reservation was located, who spoke strongly against restoration and made comments that the Paiutes and others felt were racist. The lessee of the Shivwits grazing land also spoke in opposition.

Bruce Parry and Mary Ellen Sloan made a whirlwind tour of southern Utah, meeting with the Paiute bands, prior to House hearings on the restoration bill (H.R. 4996) on October 17, 1979, in order to gather statistics on the current socioeconomic status of the Paiutes. This information helped to document their deplorable condition after termination. This brief survey concluded that Paiute per capita income was $1,968, in contrast to the $7,004 per capita income of the average citizen of Utah.

A serious lobbying effort by the Paiute Restoration Committee, with the aim of including a reservation plan in the restoration legislation, culminated when Jo Jo Hunt, staff attorney for the Senate Select Committee on Indian Affairs, developed a series of fifteen amendments to the Hatch bill that included a provision for new reservation lands to be selected and presented to Congress within two years of restoration (Hunt 1979). Committee Chair Melcher approved this version, and it was adopted through the acquiescence of Senator Hatch; even with the provision for a reservation plan, he did not kill the bill.

Despite initial opposition from the Office of Management and Budget, which had asked for further study without offering any money to fund it, the Restoration Act, Public Law 96-227, was signed by President Carter and became law on April 3, 1980.

The Reservation Phase

The Paiutes received local support for the restoration of the trust relationship, but when it came to their receiving reservation lands, such support often ended or became covert. Throughout the entire reservation planning process, it was made abundantly clear that the

Paiutes had the support of the local Bureau of Indian Affairs person-nel. This support began at the Phoenix Area Office and was espe-cially strong at the Paiute Restoration Project Office (headed by Dee Wilcox), which was established at Cedar City in November 1980, in order to implement the restoration legislation. On June 1, 1983, In-terior Secretary Watt signed DM-130, giving final approval for the Cedar City office to become a field station serving all of the Paiutes in Utah, Arizona, and Nevada. Full-scale operations began on October 1, 1983, when the field station began to function as a Southern Paiute miniagency (Holt fieldnotes, Wilcox Interview, September 15, 1983).

The Restoration Act required the secretary of the interior to present proposed legislation for a reservation to the Congress by April 3, 1982. The Paiutes were faced with a Herculean task, as they had to elect a six-member interim council, establish a membership roll, write a tribal constitution and bylaws, and then elect a council under the con-stitution. An interim council was elected on May 31, 1980, and a constitution was adopted by the tribe on October 1, 1981, and ap-proved by the secretary of the interior on October 8, 1981. An official tribal membership roll listing 503 members was finished by August 1981. Reservation planning began under the interim council with a September 1980 meeting with Utah Governor Scott Matheson. The interim council was replaced by the newly elected tribal council on October 24, 1981 (Paiute Indian Tribe of Utah 1981, 1982). The fact that they were able to accomplish all of this within such a compressed time frame is a tribute to their leaders and to their hard work.

The strongest voice in the new tribal council was that of the chair-person, Travis Benioh. The Kanosh and Indian Peaks representatives were the next most vocal and assertive members. Most issues were settled by consensus; occasionally settling an issue required a contested vote. If council members felt that they were going to lose on a vote, they often abstained, clearly desiring that unanimity be reached before proceeding to a vote. There was a conscious effort to avoid hostility between the council members and also, if at all possible, between the council and any individual Paiute constituent. Controversial measures often elicited only silence from the council members. On one occasion the silence of the council led Travis Benioh to remark: "People say I run the tribal council but I think you guys have a lot of power—

you've come down on me before—but you guys have to talk up" (Holt fieldnotes February 14, 1983).

In February of 1981, CH2M Hill, an Oregon-based consulting firm that had planned a similar (three-thousand-acre) reservation for the Siletz tribe, was retained by the Paiutes to aid in land selection and economic development. At a tribal retreat in Salt Lake City, held on February 28 and March 1, 1981, three priorities and goals for the reservation plan were established:

1. To provide a land base for the four virtually landless bands by means of which income could be generated and where job facilities could be constructed.

2. To provide a long-term source of income, jobs, management experience, and services for the tribe.

3. To provide special lands with cultural or traditional value as tribal gathering places. (Holt fieldnotes August 12, 1982)

Land selection was a strategic nightmare for the Paiutes. Virtually all of the good land in southern Utah was in private hands. Bureau of Land Management lands were marginal and, while Forest Service lands contained valuable minerals, they were either leased to or under the watchful eye of powerful interests.

With only 503 members, the Paiute population was small and destitute, and it seldom voted. It could be ignored by both local politicians and the congressional delegation. The Paiute strategy based on the concept of legislative advocacy, was dictated by powerlessness and the traditional search for consensus. Therefore in their view, it was necessary to keep as low a political profile as possible while amassing support from key white leaders, based on the moral argument that they had been badly wronged by termination. This argument shifted any blame for their condition away from the local communities to the federal government—a traditional scapegoat in this conservative part of Utah.

Their approach also played upon the Mormon population's traditional paternalistic attitudes and image of the Indian as both degraded and "worthy of help." Certain Mormon leaders were asked to help with the reservation effort as the morally right thing to do, with the end objective of raising the "level" and living standard of the Paiutes. Members of the restoration committee avoided official Mormon church hierarchical channels and communicated their concerns directly to the presidency of the church and the Quorum of the Twelve Apostles. Church leaders such as Dale Tinney and others played a crucial role in convincing local church members that the Paiutes should be allowed reservation lands. Emphasis necessarily had to be given to the Paiutes' desire for self-sufficiency and the need for good reservation land in order to accomplish this goal. Pressure was brought to bear on the Utah congressional delegation and local political leaders during this phase through personal visits, editorials, letters, and phone calls.

The role of the Paiutes' attorney was crucial during the restoration and reservation phases. Mary Ellen Sloan explained her attitude in this manner:

> I had two goals: one was to make sure that they were informed as well as they could be about all of the options that they had available to them; and secondly, I wanted to avoid influencing them about what their decisions should be, although I think that I probably told them what I thought was best. But I always felt that it was real important that they make the decisions—that it was their lives and the lives of their future—their kids. So my approach was to make it so that they could make the best, and most informed decision that they could. I think that I was not viewed as being real aggressive in terms of aggressively stating my opinion—I thought that they should reach decisions through consensus. (Holt fieldnotes, Sloan Interview, May 23, 1986).

Tribal Chairperson Travis Benioh had clearly expressed the tribal council's attitude and planning philosophy when he stated that:

> The first thing we did was eliminate private lands (except for 36 acres in Cedar City that the Indian Village stood on) out of consideration for the people who own them now.
>
> Instead we looked at lands which are the *least controversial* [emphasis added], and decided that BLM (Bureau of Land Management) lands were. However, after some research, we found that

the BLM lands in the five county area were the poorest in the
state, so we began looking at forest lands, which are more feasible
for the tribe's economic development.

Our purpose is to develop ourselves and become self-sufficient
—and we need good lands in order to accomplish this. But we're
trying to accommodate all concerns and questions, so we can do it
in the least controversial way we can. We've gone out of our way
to meet with cities, state government, the Governor, the delegations in Washington, the OMB, the Department of Interior and
the local unit of the forest service. (Cedar City Spectrum 1981)

One parcel of land originally considered for the reservation consisted of five thousand acres of National Forest land, east of the town of
Parowan. Parowan residents reacted negatively when they found that
land up their canyon was under consideration by the tribe. The fight
against inclusion in the reservation was led by Hal Mitchell, who decided to fight the proposal "tooth and nail," since his company owned
a pipeline that ran through the land to Yankee Reservoir (Holt fieldnotes, December 12, 1981). At a December 16, 1981, meeting of the
Parowan City Council, Mitchell presented a resolution opposing the
inclusion of the land in any reservation.

This meeting was attended by about one hundred Parowan residents
and representatives of the Paiute Tribe, the BIA, and CH2M Hill.
This strong opposition of local whites to granting good land to the
Paiutes was the harbinger of implacable resistance by groups with so
much political and economic power that no strategy of legislative advocacy by the essentially powerless Paiutes, no matter how brilliant,
could prevail.

As white opposition to reservation planning mounted, the support
of Senator Hatch waned. Ron Madsen, a Hatch aide who appeared at
a Parowan town meeting to repair Hatch's damaged image with local
whites, encountered the following response from Worth Grimshaw,
mayor of Enoch, who likened termination to a foolish business deal:
"The town of Enoch voted in their city council meeting that the Paiutes should not be given land. If other residents of communities made
foolish business deals, their land is not returned to them" (Cedar City
Spectrum 1982).

Opposition to the Paiute acquisition of land in Parowan was coupled with opposition to the Indians being given special treatment not available to the general population, being "given something for nothing" (Cedar City Spectrum 1982). The general white perception was that the Indians were being given land, not that the land was being restored to its rightful ownership; also involved was the Mormon tenet that some form of work is necessary in order to receive welfare. A white former president of the Cedar Indian Branch of the Mormon church stated that:

> I am convinced the Paiutes have been depressed by both church and government action in being given too much for too little in return. One of the first steps we took was to change the welfare services from a dole, and implement the return aspect of the church policy that goes with welfare programs. In that if they got commodities they knew that they were expected to do something for it. (Holt fieldnotes, Hansen interview, September 15, 1983)

Opposition to the Paiutes being "given" land was soon expressed in political pressure on Hatch. One white resident reported that Senator Hatch's support "has gone to zero in this area." Several references were made to Hatch's meeting at Southern Utah State College, in Cedar City (August 29, 1979), in which "it was made clear that the residents of the area didn't like the idea [of restoration]" (Iron County Record 1982). And yet the version of the bill that Hatch presented at the Cedar City meeting did not include the reservation plan of Section 7.

Local whites were so adamantly against the land east of Parowan being included in a reservation that the Paiutes, after meeting with Governor Matheson, dropped that parcel of land from their plan, as well as parcels near Meadow and St. George. Two other parcels also proved controversial; these were both located on Forest Service land.

The first was 430 acres of land situated on the south shore of Fish Lake, which had been a traditional subsistence area for the Koosharem band. A Sun Dance had also been held there in about 1930 by Amos Frank. The tribe wanted this land for its traditional value and as a gathering place. The second parcel, and the one with the most formidable opposition, consisted of 9,520 acres of primarily unleased coal lands. The USGS considered that about sixty-eight million tons of this coal was recoverable (Proposed PITU Reservation Plan 1982:125). Coastal States Energy Corporation's subsidiary, Southern Utah Fuel Company, leased 160 acres of this land and opposed the Paiutes' acquisition of the parcel with all the considerable political and economic clout at their disposal.

Coastal States Energy was the largest employer and a major source of tax revenue in Sevier County. The Sevier County Commission, with strong ties to Coastal States, opposed any reservation plan for the Paiutes. One of their voiced concerns was the potential loss of county taxes if almost ten thousand acres of land were designated as reserved for the Paiutes.

The tribe proposed either to implement a payment-in-lieu-of-taxes plan or a special taxing scheme to repay Sevier County for any services rendered on reservation lands. The intransigence of both Sevier County and Coastal States appears to have stemmed from no legitimate problems, but rather from: the politically conservative backgrounds of powerful key individuals; an unwillingness to grant any special status to any Indians; the attitude that "something for nothing" is immoral; an unstated desire to dismantle the Ute Reservation and all special services and privileges accorded to the Utes; and a fear that the terminated mixed-blood Utes might follow the example of the Paiutes.

Attitudes were also negative toward a reservation in the Richfield area. The conditions of the Koosharem band in Richfield had always been among the worst of any of the Paiute bands. But an April 20 editorial in the *Richfield Reaper* attacked the reservation plans and the Paiutes' strongest supporter, Congressman Dan Marriott:

> The whole thing smells of Congressional pipedreaming, and at a huge cost to the public. We do not disagree that the Indians have been mistreated in their dealings with the government. But this type of compensation will not restore to the tribe what they lost, nor will it serve the rest of the American taxpayers who will have to foot the bill for the compensation.
>
> And especially, for Dan Marriott—typical fashion for the Wasatch Front—to stick his nose into an area which he doesn't

even represent, is also disgusting. We didn't hear of Marriott offering to provide 450 acres of Snowbird Ski resort nor at the ZCMI Center where Indians also once roamed.

The paper seemed willing to admit that the government had mistreated the Indians, but not that the local community had any responsibility! As the editorial noted, redistricting by the Republican-controlled Utah State Legislature had changed Dan Marriott's district from southern Utah to the Salt Lake City area. He was thus more immune to political criticism from opponents of the reservation plan than was Senator Hatch.

While the restoration legislation called for land selection from "available public land," the Forest Service and other opponents maintained that forest lands were not "available." But in 1956 Uinta National Forest land had been returned to the Ute tribe, and in 1974, 100,000 acres of National Forest land had been put in trust for the Havasupai (Salt Lake Tribune 1982).

The proposed reservation plan consisted of seven parcels with a total of 10,000 acres of National Forest land and 4,800 acres of BLM land. The draft was endorsed by the governor of Utah, the Utah State Board of Indian Affairs, the National Congress of American Indians, the Board of Iron County Commissioners, and the Cedar City Town Council. The Joseph Town Board vigorously opposed the draft plan (Parcel 4 lay west of Joseph). The Joseph Town president said that his board opposed the plan because "of the type of environment it would bring." The opposition included the U.S. Forest Service, the Sevier County Commissioners, Coastal States Coal, the Utah Cattlemen's Association, and various individuals. An intense lobbying effort was waged by Coastal States and the congressional delegations from other coal-producing states against including Parcel 7, in eastern Sevier County (see figure 4). This effort was directed at the Utah delegation, the governor of Utah, and most importantly, at the U.S. Department of the Interior.

The original land-selection draft was essentially gutted by an opinion issued on May 7, 1982, by the interior department solicitor, William H. Coldiron, stating that the only federal lands available for

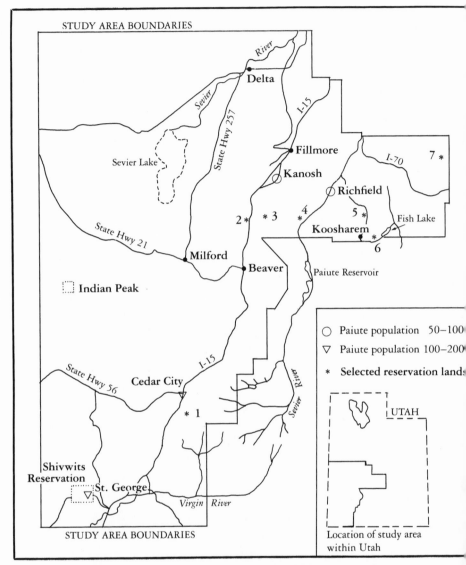

Figure 4. *Sites Selected for the Final Reservation Plan*

reservation selection were BLM lands. This was a severe blow to the tribe, as the economic potential of available BLM lands was extremely limited:

> Generally, where an economic resource, such as minerals or water, has been identified in the past, the land has been sold, traded, homesteaded, or is under patented mining claims.
>
> Basically, the BLM lands were what was left over after all the good land was taken. (U.S. Senate 1983:55)

William Cohen, then chair of the Senate Select Committee on Indian Affairs, wrote to Secretary of the Interior James Watt:

> Although I do not intend to go into great detail at this time, I will note that the Opinion fails to employ the canon of construction requiring that statutes for the benefit of Indian tribes be liberally construed in their favor. The Opinion also does not contrast the term "public" with the term "private" in section 7(c). These words appear with the term "state" and together they give meaning to the term "lands". Such an analysis would demonstrate that the public lands eligible under the bill were referred to in contrast to private or state lands and should be read in that context. No further limitation was intended. Finally, by restricting the land eligible under the Act to Bureau of Land Management land, the Opinion misses the intent of Congress, implicit throughout the Act, that the tribe should receive land that holds the promise of greater economic self-sufficiency for the tribe. The BLM lands in the area are not of sufficient quality to meet this goal. (Cohen 1982)

The Coldiron decision resulted in two separate plans being prepared for Congress, one of which still included the Forest Service Lands and thus was not acceptable to the interior department.

Unsuccessful attempts were made by the Paiute Committee for Self Determination to have the solicitor's decision withdrawn (Holt fieldnotes, July 12, 1982). But they were successful in getting the critical support of Morris Udall and the staff of the Senate and House Indian committees. Faced with the Coldiron decision, the tribal council met on February 14, 1983, to discuss five options. These options were to be forwarded to the congressional staffs for consideration and refinement.

The first two options were essentially the existing plan, one with the tribe receiving 25 percent of revenue from the coal royalties and bonuses, for an estimated annual income of $950,000 for forty years; while the other called for the tribe to receive 15 percent royalties and bonuses for an estimated annual income of $600,000 per year. The problem with the first two options was not only the Coldiron decision, but the fact that if no company decided to develop the land the Paiutes would be left with no income. Even if a company leased the land, the actual time frame of development and coal extraction was unknown.

The third option called for a payment of $2.5–5 million and the awarding of parcels 1–6 in the existing reservation plan, while excluding the coal-bearing National Forest land. The fourth option provided for $5 million and no land. The discussion in the tribal council meeting was even more muted than usual, and I noted in my fieldnotes that "the intervening months since the election appear to have taken the fight out of everyone but Travis—who seems ready to get more aggressive." (Holt fieldnotes February 14, 1983) A final option was to have the Utah congressional delegation come up with an alternative offer to the tribe.

Both Mike Jackson, the CH2M Hill representative, and Dee Wilcox, of the BIA, pushed alternative three as the most realistic and the least likely to draw the displeasure of the Utah congressional delegation.

The council members now appeared to be resigned to take whatever was offered to them; their mood was one of melancholy powerlessness. The Paiute tribal council found itself in the familiar position of taking something with the assumption that it was better than nothing. It was at this point that their dependency relationship was most apparent. Paternalistic urges in both Utah and Washington had presented them with the potential for land and money that would make a minimal improvement in their lives. Yet the structural constraints were such that they were unable to create a bill that would allow for a breakthrough to self-sufficiency.

It was the third alternative, proposed by Congressman Dan Marriott's staff, which was eventually incorporated into a compromise reservation plan and presented to Congress as H.R. 2898. The major strength of the compromise, from the tribe's point of view, was that it provided them with an assured perpetual income from the interest generated by the $2.5 million. Disadvantages included the fact that the land acquired by the tribe was of low quality and of little value. The Fish Lake parcel was also National Forest land and could not be transferred to trust status. The best compromise achievable for the Paiutes was for the tribe to be granted "exclusive use" of a portion of the south shore of Fish Lake for two weeks in June and two weeks in September of each year.

The town of Joseph still opposed the inclusion of Parcel 4, and only considerable informal pressure from Mormon sources caused them to drop their opposition. After a study by CH2M Hill and input from the state department of health, a compromise agreement was reached, which included an agreement to site any developments 1,500 feet away from the city well; to consult with Joseph on any potential development; and to install an appropriate waste-water treatment system.

In the end H.R. 2898 provided the Utah Paiutes with 4,770 acres of land, less than one-third of what the restoration legislation allowed them to select. The low quality of BLM land ruled out agricultural development, and potential commercial development was limited to concerns that could readily utilize existing tribal skills and labor. In the period from 1982 to 1983, the enterprises most often mentioned were sewing operations, gas stations and truckstops, and other tourist-oriented enterprises, such as a campground. Except for the Koosharem band land, the parcels of BLM land selected were all adjacent to interstate highways 15 and 70, with easy access for potential travelers and tourists.[2]

Parcels were to be held in trust for each of the four bands. Shivwits did not receive any additional land, as its original landbase of 27,000 acres had remained intact during the termination era. Because the National Forest lands had been deleted, no land was selected for joint tribal use.

Originally H.R. 2898 called for a $2.5-million fund for economic development. During meetings held in Cedar City and Richfield, on May 27, 1983, the tribe voiced its desire to split the fund into economic-development and tribal-services segments. H.R. 2898 was amended to allow 50 percent of the interest drawn on the fund to be utilized for tribal government. The legislation mandated that the original $2.5 million could not be touched, but that only the interest could be utilized by the tribe for economic development or tribal services. The $2.5-million trust fund was threatened by a 10 percent budget cut, but through the legislative efforts of the Paiutes and with the help of Secretary Morris Udall, these funds were restored.

The Paiute restoration occurred under the tenure of President Jimmy Carter, but the reservation phase took place during the budget-cutting of the Reagan administration and under the cloud of the Gramm-Rudman budget-balancing legislation. The Reagan administration had vetoed earlier Pequot legislation, on the grounds that the state should put up one-half of the proposed Pequot trust fund. Thus the Office of Management and Budget did not support the Paiute or any other Indian land bill. Here the advocacy of the Paiute Restoration Committee played a key role in reversing the administration's opposition. A member of the committee, with personal connections to Edwin Meese III, counselor to the president, was able to persuade the administration to support the lands bill (Meese 1983). This was the first time that Reagan's Office of Management and Budget supported any Indian land bill.

On February 17, 1984, President Reagan signed H.R. 2898, transferring 4,770 acres of land to be held in trust for the various Utah Paiute bands and authorizing a trust fund of $2.5 million. Why did the Paiute settle for less than 5,000 acres of marginal BLM land, when the original restoration legislation called for up to 15,000 acres? They were really extraordinarily lucky to have received any lands, given the forces arrayed against them during the reservation phase. The Paiute Restoration Committee appears to have used every legislative angle to produce the best possible outcome, given their power base, the attitude of the Reagan administration, and the hostility of the coal interests. Dee Wilcox, head of the BIA Cedar City office and of the restoration effort, stated that:

A tremendous amount of work was done to identify productive land but there was not much that would mean income for them.

You have to feel good about them getting something. If they get $2.5 million that's certainly better than just 5000 acres of land. . . . You have to be a little disappointed that they didn't get the big acreage that they were looking for. (Holt fieldnotes, June 10, 1986)

Another question might be: Why didn't they follow the example of the Western Shoshonis regarding their land claims and refuse to settle? Again, given the prevailing atmosphere, a court-oriented approach would, in all probability, have netted them what the Western (Temoak) Shoshonis received—exactly nothing. The consensus within the tribal council was that something, in this case the land and the trust fund, is better than nothing. The lands they received were indeed "better than nothing," but the unanswered question remains as to why the political and economic system offered them such a limited choice of alternatives: no land or only the land that no white individual or corporation wanted.

6 BEYOND
the
B I A
The Paiute Future

THE RESTORATION AND reservation process finally gave the Paiutes the opportunities that had always been available to nonterminated tribes. Nevertheless they still have a long period of work ahead of them to make up for the twenty-three years of termination. For the contemporary Paiutes, the basic policy issues are food, shelter, medical care, education, and jobs. Each one of these concerns brings families and individuals into contact with the tribal government, the Bureau of Indian Affairs, or other agencies of the federal and state bureaucracies, as well as the general economic situation of southern Utah.

The future of the Paiutes under the Bureau of Indian Affairs is unclear. Since restoration in 1980, the trend has been toward increased tribal responsibility for functions previously the responsibility of the BIA. As of 1989 the Southern Paiute Field Station in Cedar City was composed of seven employees and, in the case of the Utah Paiutes, its role was primarily to monitor federal funds and ensure that the trust relationship was intact. Since the Utah Paiutes contract almost all their services, the direct supervision of their lives by the BIA is minimal. The potential for increased autonomy and self-determination exists; however, the present policy climate mitigates against any dramatic structural changes either in the amount of government supervision or in the meager resources available to the Paiute leadership. There is a definite tendency for many tribal members to depend heavily on tribal government and services. Policy issues and the existing apparatus serve to define the social reality and place of the still-dependent Paiutes (Bee 1981).

The Paiute tribal government acts as a surrogate for the BIA and has become the focal point for Paiute aspirations and frustrations. One tribal leader remarked that "since these programs came back into being it seems like the more you gave, the more they wanted. But it shouldn't be that way. I don't want to see the tribe be another source of welfare . . . We're here to provide a service but also to help these people build their self-esteem" (Holt fieldnotes, Paiute Informant #25 1989).

The Paiute leadership of the 1980s has proved to be able and sophisticated. They have been extraordinarily served by strong leaders (within the Paiute context) and capable staff. During the restoration and reservation phases, interfamily and band conflicts were somewhat muted. During the latter part of the land-acquisition process, internal squabbles began to increase. And the departure of Travis Benioh (last name later changed to Parashonts) as tribal chairperson signaled the end of the restoration-reservation consensus.

The period from 1984 to 1990 has seen increased family conflicts that resemble the bickering of the period from 1975 to 1980. For General Anderson, tribal chairperson from 1984 to the present (1991), progress and continuity are major goals. In general tribal staff and administrators have done an admirable job; however, during 1989–90 the tribal council and staff have experienced personnel problems and several have been fired or removed. One result of the Paiutes' fixed membership is that council members are often removed and then later reelected.[1] Bee's (1990:62) description of this process among the Quechans describes the Utah Paiutes' feelings as well: "There is a prevailing notion—a tribal notion—that if someone is ousted for an alleged personal indiscretion, he or she is nonetheless "one of us" and deserves another chance—after a decent interval and apparent effort to change whatever behavior may have given offense in the first place."

The tribe employs between twenty-five and thirty individuals, and slightly less than one-half are Paiute. Since everyone is related to everyone else, the potential charge of nepotism is present with every job that is filled by a tribal member. Every job that is filled by a Paiute means that other members do not get the job and tempers often flare.

The ability to hire and not hire on what is perceived to be a fair basis is a major test of the tribal chairperson. If the majority see that the hiring is based on ability, then the conflict generated is minimal.

Tribal members come into contact with the tribal administration primarily through its health, social services, housing, and education departments. Although health care has improved dramatically since 1980, major problems still exist: 95 percent of their deaths from 1981 to 1984 were alcohol-related. The tribe has since hired an alcohol-intervention specialist. The Tribal Health Department estimated in 1984 that 68 percent of their health-care needs were not being met, and their life expectancy in 1984 was forty-two years (U.S. House of Representatives 1984). By 1989 not only were most private physicians in southern Utah available to tribal members, but there was a special clinic held at the tribal office building once a month; these have been dental, eye, diabetes, well-baby or general clinics. The attending physician would examine, prescribe, and if necessary, refer Paiute patients to specialists.

Education has held a high priority with the Paiutes since restoration.[2] They immediately hired a director of tribal education and their 1982–83 budget for education was $276,000. Prior to 1981 about 40 percent of Paiute children dropped out of school by grade eight, and only eight Paiutes had attended college in the previous ten years. The dropout rate for 1982–83 was 7.6 percent (Paiute Indian Tribe of Utah Department of Education Report 28 May 1983). By the spring of 1982, forty-four Paiutes were either attending college or vocational schools (Holt fieldnotes, Denton interview, July 16, 1982). During 1988–89 the dropout rate was 4.9 percent. As of 1989 ten Paiutes were enrolled in colleges and twelve in vocational training. Their hunger for education is evident in the fact that of those eligible (between eighteen and forty years of age), 71 percent have participated in higher education or vocational training. Unfortunately only about one in three has finished the degree or training program, and of those, only about one-half have actually been able to find work in their field (Holt fieldnotes, Paiute Informant #25 1989). Paiute students living away from home have received $225 every two weeks in addition to their tuition, books, and a $200 rent allowance. Tribal leaders have worried that, as their children graduate, they may find that the few jobs available in southern

Utah are closed to Paiutes because of prejudice. This would force the best and brightest of the young Paiutes to find work away from their traditional homeland.

Efforts towards economic development resulted in the establishment of a Paiute Economic Development Committee (PEDCO), chaired by Art Monson, the county treasurer of Salt Lake County, who is one-quarter Paiute. It was organized on March 9, 1984 (*Paiute Newsletter* March 19, 1984) and approved by the tribal council on August 23, 1984 (*Paiute Newsletter* September 21, 1984). PEDCO was successful in establishing a sewing plant at Kanosh that employs thirty to forty people (primarily Paiute women) (Holt fieldnotes, Monson interview; *Paiute Newsletter* September 30, 1985). The sewing plant has secured contracts with NASA, the U.S. Coast Guard, and commercial garment companies. In the summer of 1989, a Cedar City warehouse was refurbished to establish a second sewing plant. This building was taken into trust with no objections from the Cedar City community.[3]

Unemployment and underemployment still plagued the Paiutes in 1988, with a labor force of 137 potential workers, 77 were unemployed at some point in the year and 52 were said to be actively seeking work (Holt fieldnotes, Wilcox interview 1989). Men are more likely to be employed in the summer months. Paiute women are likely to be employed as maids in white homes, just as they have been since the 1850s. The unemployed tend to stay home and watch television, party, and "hang out." Nevertheless there is now a core of college-educated Paiute professionals (of both sexes) who can act as role models and provide an alternative to the customary poverty conditions.

The Koosharem band has begun to benefit from the Joseph parcel; five house trailers have been located there and twelve HUD homes have been built. There was a plan to build a truckstop on the frontage road, and signs on Paiute land will bring cash to the Koosharem band (Holt fieldnotes, Anderson interview 1989). The Cedar band has also leased land, south of Cedar City, for advertising signs.

The tribal administration has done an excellent job of acquiring HUD housing for tribal members. In addition to the houses at Joseph, nine new HUD homes in Cedar City and four at Shivwits were all virtually completed by July of 1989.

Toward the Future

The student of the Utah Paiutes must be careful to remember that the current Native American group designated as the Paiute Indian Tribe of Utah is an amalgamation of Pahvant, Ute/Paiute, and several remnant groups of Southern Paiutes. These amalgamated groups have historical identities that exacerbate cleavages within the tribe. The Utah Paiutes have never been a homogeneous nation: family, faction, and band affiliations create centrifugal pressures. The Cedar band, for example, currently contains two family-based factions. The Kanosh band is often seen by other Paiutes as a source of trouble, since they tend to avoid consensus and attempt to go their own way.

The fight for restoration and then reservation lands provided a reason for the Utah Paiutes to present a united front. But by the end of 1984, differences, apparently based on personality and family conflicts, seemed to be on the increase, and the departure of Travis Benioh (Parashonts) as tribal chairperson signaled the end of the restoration/ reservation consensus. Criticism of whomever holds tribal offices is a given. Paiute political life is based on family-centered loyalties, and the most vocal families often have their way in a political confrontation; family cleavages remain more important than band identification. The pressures on the Utah Paiutes to feud among themselves appear to be strong and dangerous. Internal problems have tended to slow socio-economic development and may well cause serious problems in the future.

The LDS church is still the major nongovernmental force in the Paiutes' lives, and Mormon paternalism still seeks to mold their lives for "their own good." The current political situation is subject to some limited control by the Paiutes, if they appeal to certain ideological themes understandable by the Mormon population. Both the present research and the literature suggest, however, that the unequal position of power occupied by the Paiutes also means that such control will serve only limited goals and provide only limited opportunities for autonomy and self-determination. The Utah Paiutes have traditionally exploited multiple membership roles as an ethnic group and as sporadic members of the Mormon church. This strategy has allowed them to utilize resources made available from both the federal government and the Mormon church. Even non-Mormon Paiutes have been able to utilize resources made available to their Mormon relatives. Since the extended family units share risks and resources, they have adapted and yet have been able to avoid assimilation.

The Mormon church has been and remains the major vehicle for upward social mobility for individual Paiutes. As a tribe their successful bid to regain trust status depended upon the support of the Utah congressional delegation and Mormon church leaders. In turn, this support rested on two assumptions: that termination was an incorrect federal action, leaving the Paiutes to suffer as a result; and that the religious duty of the Mormon population of Utah is to "help" the Indians. Paternalism has been a two-edged sword; it helped create the dependency and other problems of the Paiutes, yet the fact that the relationship of dependency existed also allowed them to call upon their white sympathizers for help.

In order to assimilate the Indian into a homogeneous life-style that conforms to the Mormon world view, one of the primary goals of the Mormons has been to destroy the culture of the Paiutes. This was to be accomplished by teaching them to dress, live, and act like the Mormons. Such a goal is still a high priority among Mormons working with the contemporary Paiute. Although dances and feathers are viewed favorably as "culture," the traditional ideology, world views, and social practices are seen as either superstition or antiprogressive.

Despite concerted efforts to destroy their culture and to transform their minds and lives, the Paiutes remain an identifiable people. Boundaries are continually maintained between them and their Anglo neighbors. Anglos are seen as users, liars, people who tell you what you want to hear and hold back their real intentions and emotions. And the Anglo view is that the Paiutes are ignorant, dirty, lazy, and stupid. As Spicer (1971:797) has shown, for a people to be overwhelmed, yet still persist, they must walk a fine line: they must offer sufficient opposition to their oppressors to avoid being absorbed, yet they must be cooperative enough to avoid being the victims of genocide or wholesale destruction.

Paternalism has changed in character and perhaps declined somewhat, but it is still a major force in the lives of the Paiutes. Writing in April of 1984, one Paiute complained that "I find we haven't really been given the chance to show the world we're able to handle our problem and work alone. We're still being treated as though we are children" (*Paiute Newsletter* April 19, 1984).

The Paiutes have nevertheless become more visible throughout southern Utah. In 1981 to celebrate their restored trust status, the Paiute Indian Tribe of Utah began a Restoration Gathering in June of each year. This celebration has become the major contemporary social event in the Paiute calendar. The gathering marks the restoration of federal recognition of the Utah Paiute tribe and includes a princess pageant, a parade through downtown Cedar City, hand games, dinners, historical and educational presentations, and a softball tournament. In 1984 it was expanded from a purely Paiute event to include an intertribal powwow, featuring dance contests, drumming, and hand games. White attendance has increased slowly since the powwow began. The "Restoration Gathering and Pow Wow" provides the only major reason for local whites to observe and interact with the Paiutes, except through work or the Mormon church. The effort that goes into producing this event creates pride and solidarity among the participants. The intertribal aspects, such as the dance contests and the hand games, create an opportunity for the Paiutes to meet other Native Americans and exchange information and songs. One of the primary benefits of the Gathering is its visibility; here is an opportunity for the Paiutes to express their ethnic pride and to say to the Anglo community that they are proud of who they are, that they have not vanished, that they are still living today in their homeland.

An explicit goal in this study has been to provide a new understanding of how and why the Paiutes have arrived where they are today. During my fieldwork I was constantly told, "if you figure us out, let us know, because we don't understand ourselves." My hope is that this book will help the Paiutes and their white neighbors to understand their past and present, in order to build a better future together.

APPENDIX
Methods and Sources

MY WORK WITH the Paiutes began in 1981, when I was teaching at Southern Utah State College, in Cedar City, Utah. I was asked by Travis Benioh, then tribal chairperson, to research questions concerning the Paiute Tribe's envisioned reservation plan. It so happened that events in the Middle East had left me without a dissertation topic, so I jumped at the chance to work with an American Indian tribe. For several years I continued to do an occasional research job, serve as an ad hoc member of the Committee for Paiute Self-Determination, and act as advocate and general errand runner.

Close association with tribal members and their quest for land immediately sparked my interest in the underlying causes of Paiute poverty and underemployment. I became very curious about the origins of their current problems and of their continued reliance on local whites in general and the Mormon church in particular. I soon realized that it would be necessary to trace the historical and contemporary interactions of both the Mormon church and the Bureau of Indian Affairs with the Paiutes, in order to understand their present predicament. Confronted with a series of interrelated questions, I began to combine my activities as an advocate for the Paiutes with the standard ethnographic fieldwork techniques of the anthropologist. As I began to trace the origins of Paiute dependence, I turned to ethnohistorical materials. My research strategy stressed primary sources such as reports to the commissioner of Indian affairs, organizational minutes, letters, personal journals, and other archival materials. I paid special attention to the Palmer Collection at Southern Utah State College; the

Denver Federal Records Center; the Doris Duke Oral History Collection, at the University of Utah; the files of the American West Center, at the University of Utah; the Utah State Archives; the Utah Historical Society; The Church of Jesus Christ of Latter-Day Saints Archives; the Bureau of Indian Affairs files in Cedar City; and my own personal collection of photocopied materials that grew due to the kindness of countless individuals.

The geographic dispersion of the Paiutes across southern Utah created problems for traditional participant observation. Most of my work centered around the tribal chairperson, the tribal council, and the tribal attorney. I did, however, spend a considerable amount of time interviewing key informants from each of the five bands; nevertheless, my fieldnotes are weakest in dealing with the Shivwits and Koosharem bands. Between 1981 and 1989, I spent the majority of my field time with the members of the Indian Peaks, Kanosh, and Cedar bands. I interviewed more than fifty adult Paiutes, or about 10 percent of the total population. I also attended tribal gatherings such as tribal council meetings, Mormon church programs, picnics, and powwows.

Earlier research on the Southern Paiutes of Utah has generally either been oriented toward salvage ethnography or history and acculturation. Emphasis has often been placed on their adaptations to a particular environment and the limitations imposed upon them by that environment. John Wesley Powell conducted the first ethnographic field research with the Paiutes and other Numic-speaking Indians in the years 1868–80 (Fowler and Fowler 1971:1–34). His work was, of course, conducted during the early formative days of American anthropology. The bulk of his manuscripts were devoted to linguistics and mythological data. Other major early sources include Sapir (1910, 1930–31), Lowie (1924), Palmer (1933), and Omer Stewart (1942).

Isabel Kelly (1934, 1939, 1964) worked extensively with the Utah Paiute from 1932 to 1933, and her detailed report and various articles give us the most substantial data available concerning group composition, subsistence, religious practices, and life-style. She also created what are still the most acceptable historic boundary lines for the Southern Paiute Nation.

Julian Steward (1938) did most of his Paiute work with Nevada informants. He assumed that the harsh environment of the Basin would limit the inhabitants' capacities for elaborate social institutions, and that their pattern of technology and ritual would be very simple. Steward failed to note the extent of the changes brought on by the white presence and may have underestimated the variety of ecozones available within the Basin. Not only was the environment changed by such practices as irrigation and overgrazing, but the ability of the Paiutes to utilize the variety of resources offered by the environment was severely curtailed by white ownership of the land. Thus in the postcontact situation, the human environmental limitations may have been a much more significant factor in the adaptation of the Southern Paiutes than was the natural environment.

Euler (1966) has outlined the major ethnohistorical references to the Paiute and makes some mention of the process of acculturation. A close look at Euler is very instructive in illustrating the serious gaps in our knowledge of the Paiutes. These gaps, often of many years, combined with the uneven quantity and quality of the sources for the time periods that are at least partially documented, create real problems in understanding postcontact Paiutes. It also becomes clear that much of what had been taken to be the "pristine" Paiute precontact culture probably actually represented the first phases of adaptation to the coming of the whites (Alley 1982).

Braithwaite (1972), in a two-volume dissertation, compared the development of political leadership among the Paiutes of Cedar City to that of the Paiutes on the Kaibab Reservation, just across the Utah-Arizona border. Braithwaite also offered some important data on the influence of local Mormon church officials on the life-style and decision-making processes of the Paiutes, especially in Cedar City. Braithwaite often referred to Mormon paternalistic attitudes, but he failed to integrate his observations into any coherent theoretical framework.

Anne Spencer (1973) has provided us not only with a short history of the Cedar City Paiutes, but has also given us a unique look at both the effects of a major federal program and Mormon-Paiute relations in the early 1970s. This internship report discussed the impact of the VISTA program on the Cedar band, outlined the Paiute educational situation, and reported on the extent of prejudice and hostility between the Paiutes and the Mormons.

Mary Jacobs (1974) presented the most complete descriptive account of the withdrawal of federal services to the Paiute during the 1950s as well as some information about the effects of the federal policy of termination.

In 1976 the Inter-Tribal Council of Nevada published a history of the Paiutes of Nevada and Utah; but this brief account was oriented toward high-school students and, valuable as it is, only offered a general history of the Utah bands. Even so it remains an excellent source with which to begin an investigation of their relations with the federal government.

Martha Knack's work (1980) on the household organization of the Utah Paiutes is virtually the only in-depth treatment of these people since the termination era. This excellent study documented the adaptations of Paiute social and kinship organization to the conditions of poverty and neglect they faced prior to restoration. Knack documented a particular response of the Paiutes to their dependent status, thereby revealing both resistance against and adaptation to that condition.

Kelly and Fowler (1986) attempted to present an encyclopedic summary of current knowledge on Southern Paiutes in the Great Basin volume of the *Handbook of North American Indians*. Their work is an excellent point of departure for the scholar or layperson interested in pursuing the subject.

Pamela Bunte and Robert Franklin (1987) dealt with the effects of Navajo expansion into Paiute country and the ethnohistory of the San Juan Paiutes. Franklin and Bunte (1990) is a brief introduction to the Southern Paiutes centered on the Kiabab and San Juan groups.

John Alley (1986) discussed the joint efforts of tribal governments and the University of Utah's American West Center to publish tribal histories authored by or containing major contributions by native basin people. As yet no Southern Paiute ethnohistorian has come forward to tell the story of his or her people, but we look to that day with anticipation.

NOTES

Introduction

1. Dependency theory emerged from the work of Baran (1957) and Frank (1969). As it is currently used, dependency is not a label for a unified theoretical position, but a term for an umbrella of ideas about inequality. Nonetheless those interested in the phenomenon generally share the premise that the structure of international world capitalism is one of inequality, where the centers of advanced capitalism (metropolitan/core) stand in a relationship of domination, exploitation, and control over the less-developed (peripheral/dependent) areas. Thus the world is seen as a series of asymmetrical vertical relationships between the independent, controlling areas and those areas of the world that are dependent and controlled.

2. Federal policies toward Native Americans have always been a form of planned social change. Indian policy was, and is, implemented so that the future might be different in ways perceived as desirable by the policy makers. In Indian affairs that "desirable future" has been defined by a raw consensus of white opinion and implemented through the plenary power of Congress.

A critical element of public policy, not only in Indian affairs but in all sectors, has been its incremental nature. New policies are built on the existing structures and ideological consensuses, and these new policies are usually only marginally different from either previous or alternative policies. Thus instead of public policy being the result of an objective or rational-comprehensive view of goals and opportunities, it is often the "science of muddling through" (Lindblom 1959:79–88). This incremental characteristic of public policy not only makes value-free evaluation difficult, if not impossible, but also allows for unstated ideological assumptions to become the foundation of policy.

Anthropologists dealing with these issues have noted the contradictory effects of policy on local groups (C. Smith 1978).

Chapter 1

1. For more information concerning the Southern Paiute language, see Sapir (1930–31) and Bunte (1979).

2. During my fieldwork I also took advantage of the climatic variation: I could go skiing during the morning, in the mountains east of Cedar City, and then, descending as I drove south, was able to sunbathe and swim with temperatures in the 80s at Redcliffs, near St. George.

3. For a good overview of social organization in the Great Basin, see Fowler (1966).

4. Palmer (1936) suggests that the Paiutes figured descent through the mother's line and that they practiced matrilocal postmarital residence. My view is that they probably preferred matrilocal residence, until the coming of the whites began to put emphasis on the labor of Paiute men. Thus the difference between what Kelly recorded (instances of patrilocal residence) and the cultural ideal of matrilocal residence represented an adaptation to white domination of the Paiutes' political and physical environment.

5. For other significant material of ethnographic importance, see appendix.

6. For more information on the band debate, see Steward (1970: 147) and C. Fowler (1982b: 132).

7. A term associated with the Piede of the Cedar City area is *mungwa* (variant of Nungwu?), while the early "Pahute" (at least on the Santa Clara) are said by Hamlin (1854–57:19) to refer to themselves as Yannawants. An exception to the foraging emphasis of the Piede is Toquer's band, referred to as Piede, yet clearly engaged in horticulture. Piedes are mentioned as being from "the desert," from Beaver, from the Cedar City area, Harmony and Toquer's band on the north part of Ash Creek. People from the Santa Clara, Muddy, and Vegas rivers are referred to as Pahutes or Paiutes. Reports of first or early encounters with Paiutes tend to use Piede to include all Paiutes, and this may account for Toquer's band being referred to as Piede. As the early chroniclers became more familiar with the Paiute situation, they tended to differentiate between the two groups.

8. Bunte and Franklin (1987) have presented the best available view of the early modern impact of traditional religion. Although they deal primarily with the San Juan Paiutes, there is some information included from Bunte's work with the Kaibab.

9. One of the cry singers is a Walapai (Hualapai) man. Some of the Paiutes often visit Walapai "relatives" at Peach Springs and consider themselves to be closely related to the Walapai. Spier (1928) also noted interaction between Paiutes and the Walapai. This relationship deserves closer scrutiny.

10. Mormon attitudes toward Indians were similar to those of other denominations; for the Mormons, however, converting and civilizing them was essential for the last days to come. This belief in the necessity of Indian conversions has been a major theological difference between Mormons and other Christians. For an overview of the Mormon mission impulse, see Peterson (1975).

Chapter 2

1. The reformers were generally churchmen, who advocated a more "humanitarian style" of assimilation based on education, Christianity, and the dismemberment of tribalism. Prucha (1986:198) refers to the reform period as "a high point of paternalism."

2. The BIA agent Lorenzo Creel apparently filed on new and contiguous lands sometime prior to 1915, thus giving each Indian 160 acres and providing land for fifteen other Indians (McConihe 1915).

3. Mormon missionary work during this period with the Indians in Utah occurred on an ad hoc basis. Generally a local white, such as William Palmer, in Cedar City, and the non-Mormon Frank Beckwith, in Delta, became interested in the Indian culture and language. Impelled by their interest in the Indians, they then attempted to help improve the economic condition of the local group and occasionally also taught them something of Mormonism. There was no central direction of this missionary effort until the late 1940s.

4. In 1944 L. J. Arnold, of Gunnison Sugar, Inc., in Centerfield, Utah, wrote Parvin Church, inviting Indian families to come for the beet harvest that started on October 9. Arnold said that he would pay their gas bill to and from work and/or send a truck down to pick up the Paiutes (Arnold 1944). In 1949 the concern of local Richfield citizens for the welfare of the children of Indian migrant laborers would spark the LDS church's Indian Placement Program.

5. On page 15 White stated that there were thirty-two families, grouped in thirteen consumption units. I have calculated that 76 percent of this small income came from wage labor, 14 percent from pensions, relief, and agency aid, and 10 percent from reservation sources, such as income from livestock and timber. The average income in this case may be quite misleading, since

White (1946b:19) stated that 91 of the total of 121 Shivwits had incomes of less than $200.

Chapter 3

1. Watkins had grown up near the Ute reservation in north-central Utah and had apparently always viewed the solution to the "Indian problem" as being something akin to the Dawes Act (see Thompson 1983). Another Mormon who played a major role in termination was Rex Lee, associate commissioner Indian Affairs. Lee went on to hold major federal government posts and to become president of Brigham Young University.

2. The 1952 report indicates how termination descended upon the Paiutes like a "bolt from the blue." In 1952 nothing was being done to prepare them for withdrawal, in 1954 they were terminated, and in 1957 the withdrawal process was over.

3. Carriker (1978:26–31) discusses how the Kalispel settlement was used in an attempt to blackmail that tribe into accepting termination.

4. For a discussion of termination as attempted genocide, see Drinnon 1987:242–43 and 317.

Chapter 4

1. For an excellent, short overview of the ICC, see Rosenthal (1985); see also Lurie (1978).

2. See Congressional Record (May 20, 1946):5307–16.

3. For a positive view of the Indian claims process by a partner of the Wilkinson, Cragun and Barker firm, see Glen A. Wilkinson, 1966. Charles Wilkinson (no relation to Glen or Ernest) discusses the ethical problems of the ICC in Philp, ed., 1986:151–55.

4. See United States v. Sioux Nations, 100 S.Ct. 2715, 2726 & n. 17 (1980).

5. Chairman John Vance attempted to implement section 13b in 1968, but made no progress in the face of vested interests and twenty-two years of adversarial precedent.

6. See the fall 1955 edition of Ethnohistory; see also Beals (1985) and Lurie (1985).

7. Wilkinson worked as president of BYU with no salary for the first thirteen years. He lived on his income from the law firm, which "sometimes totaled more than $100,000 annually" (Bergera and Priddis 1985:24).

8. Despite Robert Barker's assertions to the contrary (Gottlieb and Wiley 1984:172), I have seen no written evidence that suggests that the Wilkinson

firm opposed the concept of termination. Wilkinson's testimony before the joint congressional subcommittees considering termination indicate that Glen Wilkinson was not comfortable with the termination of the Paiutes at that time (U.S. Congress 1954:86). Another member of the Wilkinson firm, Carl Hawkins, stated in a telephone interview, that the firm opposed termination and attempted to defeat it initially. However when it became apparent that Senator Watkins would steamroll the legislation, they turned to a strategy of damage control and mitigation (Holt Fieldnotes, Carl Hawkins interview, 1991). Glen Wilkinson assisted with both the Klamath and Menominee withdrawal programs; these two groups were general clients of the firm, and Wilkinson estimated (G. Wilkinson 1955) that they would provide the two largest sources of nonclaims income to the firm during 1955.

9. See House Hearings on H.R. 1198 and H.R. 1341, 79th Congress (U.S. House of Representatives 1945) and House Report 1466, p. 10. See also *United States v. Alcea Band of Tillamooks,* 329 U.S.40, 51–2 (1946). The Wilkinson firm filed *amicus curiae* briefs in the Tee-Hit-Ton, the Tillamook, and in the *Pawnee Tribe of Oklahoma v. United States* cases.

10. In 1956 the Miamis were awarded $.75 an acre for land they had lost in 1818. They appealed and were given $1.15 per acre, in 1960.

11. Ernest Wilkinson's actual work on the Southern Paiute claims appears to have been minimal and essentially administrative. The Southern Paiute case really began in 1948 and ended in 1965; perhaps twenty attorneys worked on some segment of the case. My reading of the documents indicates that Donald Gormley carried the largest share of the workload. Mr. Cragun played a key role in the September 12, 1961, hearing before the ICC. Mrs. Horn drafted the original findings of fact and evaluated the rough value of the Paiute claims and the probable government offsets. John Boyden did some of the original research for the petition in Docket No. 330, acted as a mediator between the firm and the Southern Paiutes, and attended numerous meetings. Mr. Boyden, Mr. Gormley, and Mrs. Horn attended the meetings at which the Paiutes were convinced to accept the compromise proposal. Mr. Abe Weissbrodt apparently did most of the work in Docket No. 88.

12. While it is true that they were inactive in the western sense, it is also clear that traditional Paiute forms of political activity continued throughout this period.

13. See Gottlieb and Wiley (1984) and also Stewart and Wiley (1981).

Chapter 5

1. See the *Salt Lake Tribune*, July 20, 1975, for an interview with Bruce Parry. This interview and an accompanying piece discussed the condition of the Paiutes in general and of the Koosharem reservation in particular.

2. During the summer of 1990, negotiations began for a truckstop to be located on one of these parcels.

Chapter 6

1. The Utah Paiute Tribal Council as of June 1990 was composed of:
General Anderson, Chair, Indian Peaks Band
Mark Snow, Vice-Chair, Shivwits Band
Vera Charles, Koosharem Band
Woodrow Pete, Cedar Band
McKay Pikyavit, Kanosh Band

2. For a discussion of the educational situation of the Utah Paiutes in 1973–74, see Martha Knack (1978).

3. The labor force at the Cedar City plant was about one-half Paiute in August 1989, when it opened.

REFERENCES CITED

Aberle, Sophie D.
  1958   Paiute Interview Notes. Ronald Holt files. Layton, Utah.
Adams, William
  1852   Letter of December 11, Deseret News.
Albers, Patricia
  1982   Sioux Kinship in a Colonial Setting. Dialectical Anthropology
         6:253–69.
  1985   Autonomy and Dependency in the Lives of Dakota Women: A
         Study in Historical Change. Review of Radical Political Economics
         17:109–34.
Albers, Patricia, and Jeanne Kay
  1985   Sharing the Land: A Study in American Indian Territoriality. Un-
         published manuscript. Ronald Holt files. Layton, Utah.
Alcorn, J. R.
  1940   Life History Notes on the Paiute Ground Squirrel. Journal of
         Mammalogy 21:160–70.
Alley, John
  1982   Prelude to Dispossession: The Fur Trade's Significance for the
         Northern Utes and Southern Paiutes. Utah Historical Quarterly
         50:104–23.
  1986   Tribal Historical Projects. In Handbook of North American Indi-
         ans: Great Basin. Ed. by Warren d'Azevedo 11:601–7.
Allred, Glade
  1957   Letter to Darrell Fleming, April 30, 1957. BIA files, Cedar City,
         Utah.
Anders, Gary

1979   The Internal Colonization of Cherokee Native Americans. Development and Change 10:41–55.

1980   Theories of Underdevelopment and the American Indian. Journal of Economic Issues 14: 681–701.

Anderson, Edward H.

1900   Apostle Lyman's Mission [1882] to the Indians. Improvement Era 3:510–16.

Anderson, James E.

1979   Public Policy Making, 2d. ed. New York: Holt, Rinehart and Winston.

Arnold, L. J.

1944   Letter to P. Church, October 2, 1944. Denver Federal Records Center, Group 75.

Artickels of Agreement

1889   Between The Indians Pogneb Bob and the Fremont Eragation Companys [*sic*]. March 1, 1889, on record at County Recorder's Office, Wayne County, Utah. Copy in Ronald Holt files. Layton, Utah.

Ashman, Dale

1957   Letter to Uintah-Ouray Realty Officer, August 7, 1957. BIA files, Cedar City, Utah.

Axtell, James

1981   The European and the Indian: Essays in the Ethnohistory of Colonial North America. Oxford: Oxford University Press.

Bagley, Edward

1926   Letter to Dr. E. A. Fairnow [Farrow]. BIA files, Cedar City, Utah.

Bailey, F. G.

1969   Stratagems and Spoils: A Social Anthropology of Politics. New York: Schocken Books.

Baran, Paul A.

1957   The Political Economy of Growth. New York: Monthly Review Press.

Barker, Robert

1956   Letter to Spencer W. Kimball. John Boyden files, Salt Lake City, Utah.

Barsh, Russel, and James Henderson

1980   The Road: Indian Tribes and Political Liberty. Berkeley: University of California Press.

Beals, Ralph

1985   The Anthropologist as Expert Witness. Pp. 19–55 in Irredeem-

able America: The Indians' Estate and Land Claims. Ed. by Imre Sutton
Albuquerque: University of New Mexico Press.

Beckwith, Frank
    1975   Indian Joe. Delta, Utah: DuWil Publishing.

Bee, Robert L.
    1979   To Get Something for the People: The Predicament of the American Indian Leader. Human Organization 38:239–47.
    1981   Crosscurrents along the Colorado: The Impact of Government Policy on the Quechan Indians. Tucson: University of Arizona Press.
    1982   The Politics of American Indian Policy. Cambridge, Mass.: Schenkman Publishing.

Berger, Peter L.
    1976   Pyramids of Sacrifice. Garden City, N.Y.: Anchor.

Bergera, Gary, and Ronald Priddis
    1985   Brigham Young University: A House of Faith. Salt Lake City: Signature Books.

Berkhofer, Robert, Jr.
    1979   The White Man's Indian. New York: Vintage Books.

Bettinger, Robert, and Martin Baumloff
    1982   The Numic Spread: Great Basin Cultures in Competition. American Antiquity 47:485–503.

Bobo, W. T.
    1956   Withdrawal Narratives. BIA files, Cedar City, Utah.

Book of Mormon
    1830   Palmyra, New York.

Braithwaite, Douglas C.
    1972   The Mastery of Cultural Contradictions: Developing Paiute Leadership. Ph.D. diss., M.I.T.

Brill, Paul
    1965   Letter to Chief Tribal Enrollment Section, May 11. BIA files, Cedar City, Utah.

Brooks, Juanita
    1944   Indian Relations on the Mormon Frontier. Utah Historical Quarterly 12:1–48.
    1962   The Mountain Meadows Massacre. Norman: University of Oklahoma Press.
    1964   On the Mormon Frontier: The Diary of Hosea Stout. Salt Lake City: University of Utah Press.
    1972   Journal of the Southern Indian Mission: Diary of Thomas D. Brown. Logan: Utah State University Press.

Brophy, William A., and Sophie D. Aberle
   1966   The Indian: America's Unfinished Business. Norman: University of Oklahoma Press.
Bunte, Pamela
   1979   Problems in Southern Paiute Syntax and Semantics. Bloomington: Indiana University, Ph.D. Diss.
Bunte, Pamela, and Robert J. Franklin
   1987   From the Sands to the Mountain: Change and Persistence in a Southern Paiute Community. Lincoln: University of Nebraska Press.
Burt, Larry W.
   1982   Tribalism in Crisis: Federal Indian Policy, 1953–1961. Albuquerque: University of New Mexico Press.
Butler, Lafollette
   1965   Letter to Wade Head, June 4. BIA files, Cedar City, Utah.
Canby, William C.
   1981   American Indian Law. St. Paul, Minn.: West Publishing.
Carriker, Robert
   1978   The Kalispel Tribe and the Indian Claims Commission Experience. Western Historical Quarterly 4: 19–31
Cave, Alfred A.
   1985   Richard Hakluyt's Savages. International Social Science Review 60: 3–24.
Cedar Board of Paiute Indians
   1967   Meeting Minutes, April 3. BIA files, Cedar City, Utah.
Cedar City Spectrum
   1981   Tribe Misunderstood by Council Benioh Says. December 9.
   1982   Paiutes Can Re-Select Land. January 12.
Chambers, Erve
   1985   Applied Anthropology: A Practical Guide. Englewood Cliffs: Prentice-Hall.
Chilcote, Ronald, ed.
   1982   Dependency and Marxism: Toward a Resolution of the Debate. Boulder: Westview Press.
Christy, Howard A.
   1978   Open Hand and Mailed Fist: Mormon-Indian Relations in Utah, 1847–52. Utah Historical Quarterly 46: 216–35.
   1979   The Walker War: Defense and Conciliation as Strategy. Utah Historical Quarterly 47: 395–420.
Church, P. E.

1944   Letter to Forrest Stone, December 16, 1944. Denver Federal Records Center, Group 75.

Cleland, Robert, and Juanita Brooks, eds.
1983   A Mormon Chronicle: The Diaries of John D. Lee, 1848–76. Salt Lake City: University of Utah Press.

Coates, Lawrence
1969   A History of Indian Education by the Mormons, 1830–1900. Ed.D. diss., Ball State University.

Cohen, Felix E.
1982   Cohen's Handbook of Federal Indian Law. Charlottesville: Bobbs-Merrill.

Cohen, Lucy, ed.
1960   The Legal Conscience: Selected Papers of Felix S. Cohen. New Haven: Yale University Press.

Cohen, Ronald
1978   Ethnicity: Problem and Focus in Anthropology. Annual Review of Anthropology 7:379–403.

Cohen, William S.
1982   Letter to James Watt, August 11, 1982. Copy in author's possession.

Condie, Leroy
1955–56   Narrative Travel Reports, December 1955–August 1956. BIA files, Cedar City, Utah.

Cowan, Richard
1979   The Kingdom is Rolling Forth. Provo: BYU Press.

Cragun, John W.
1964   Letter to Philleo Nash, December 15. John Boyden files.
1965   Letter to John Boyden, May 17. John Boyden files. Salt Lake City, Utah.

Creel, Lorenzo
1916   Letter to Commissioner of Indian Affairs. Federal Records Group 75.

Crum, Steven
1983   The Western Shoshone of Nevada and the Indian New Deal. Ph.D. diss., University of Utah.

Danforth, Sandra C.
1973   Repaying Historical Debts: The Indian Claims Commission. North Dakota Law Review 49:359–403.

Daughters of Utah Pioneers

1949   Golden Nuggets of Pioneer Days: A History of Garfield County. Panguitch, Utah: Garfield County News.

d'Azevedo, Warren et al., eds.

1966   The Current Status of Anthropological Research in the Great Basin: 1964. Reno: University of Nevada, Desert Research Institute Social Sciences and Humanities Publications 1.

1973   Some Recent Studies of Native American Political Relations in the Western Great Basin: A Commentary. Pp. 103–18 in Native American Politics: Power Relationships in the Western Great Basin Today. Ed. by Ruth M. Houghton. Reno: University of Nevada Bureau of Governmental Research.

Deloria, Vine, and Clifford Lytle

1984   The Nations Within: The Past and Future of American Indian Sovereignty. New York: Pantheon.

Deseret News

1851   Letter, December 13.

1852   Letter from William Adams, December 11.

Dibble, Charles

1947   The Mormon Mission to the Shoshoni Indians. Utah Humanities Review 1:53–73.

Drinnon, Richard

1987   Keeper of Concentration Camps: Dillon S. Myer and American Racism. Berkeley: University of California Press.

Ducheneaux, Karen

1975   Memo to Charles Worthman, July 2, 1975. Denver Federal Records Center, Group 75.

Dye, Thomas R.

1981   Understanding Public Policy, 4th ed. Englewood Cliffs: Prentice-Hall.

1987   Power and Society. Monterey, Cal.: Brooks/Cole Publishing.

Emmons, Glen

1952   Letter to Murray, June 18, 1952. BIA files, Cedar City, Utah.

England, Eugene

1985   "Lamanites" and the Spirit of the Lord. Dialogue: A Journal of Mormon Thought 18:25–32.

Esplin, Fred C., and Kevin Anderson

1982   Slow Justice: Looking for Land with the Paiutes. Utah Holiday 11:55–61.

Euler, Robert C.

1966   Southern Paiute Ethnohistory. University of Utah Anthropological Papers 78. Salt Lake City: University of Utah Press.

Evans, Joshua T.

1938   The Northern Shoshone Indians under the Ecclesiastical Administration of the Church of Jesus Christ of Latter-day Saints as Exemplified at the Washakie Colony, Utah. M.A. thesis, Utah State University.

Farrow, E. A.

1927   Letter to C. E. Faris, September 27.

1930   Letter to Commissioner of Indian Affairs, August 18.

Fixico, Donald Lee

1980   Termination and Relocation: Federal Indian Policy in the 1950s. Ph.D. diss.: University of Oklahoma.

Forbes, Jack

1974   Native Americans of California and Nevada: A Handbook. Berkeley: The Far West Laboratory for Educational Research and Development.

Foster, George

1973   Traditional Societies and Technological Change, 2d ed. New York: Harper and Row.

Fowler, Catherine S.

1982a   Food-named Groups among Northern Paiute in North America's Great Basin: An Ecological Interpretation. Pp. 113–29 in Resource Managers: North American and Australian Hunter-Gatherers. Ed. by Nancy Williams and Eugene Hunn. Boulder: American Association for the Advancement of Science, Selected Symposium 67.

1982b   Settlement Patterns and Subsistence Systems in the Great Basin: The Ethnographic Record. Pp. 121–38 in Man and Environment in the Great Basin. Ed. by David Madsen and James O'Connell. Washington, D.C.: Society for American Archaeology.

Fowler, Don D.

1966   Great Basin Social Organization. Pp. 57–73 in The Current Status of Anthropological Research in the Great Basin. Reno: University of Nevada, Desert Research Institute 1.

Fowler, Don, and Catherine S. Fowler

1971   Anthropology of the Numa: John Wesley Powell's Manuscripts on the Numic Peoples of Western North America, 1868–80. Smithsonian Contributions to Anthropology, 14.

Fowler, Loretta

1982   Arapahoe Politics 1851–1978. Lincoln: University of Nebraska Press.

Frank, André G.
   1966   The Development of Underdevelopment. Monthly Review 18:17–
      31.
   1969   Capitalism and Underdevelopment in Latin America. New York
      and London: Monthly Review Press.
   1978   World Accumulation, 1492–1789. Monthly Review Press.
   1979   Dependent Accumulation and Underdevelopment. Monthly Re-
      view Press.
Franklin, Robert, and Pamela Bunte
   1990   The Paiute. New York: Chelsea House Publishers.
Furniss, Norman F.
   1960   The Mormon Conflict. New Haven.
Gibson, Arrell M.
   1980   The American Indian: Prehistory to the Present. Lexington, Mass.:
      D. C. Heath.
Gilmore, Harry
   1953   Letter to Douglas McKay, Secretary of the Interior. September 14.
      Denver, Federal Records Center. Records Group 75.
   1954   Notice of Hearings, January 27, 1954. BIA files, Cedar City, Utah.
Glaser, Barney, and Anselm L. Strauss
   1967   The Discovery of Grounded Theory. Chicago: Aldine.
Goodell, Grace
   1985   Paternalism, Patronage, and Potlatch: The Dynamics of Giving
      and Being Given To. Current Anthropology 26:249–66.
Gormley, Donald C.
   1965   Letter to John S. Boyden, January 4. John Boyden files.
Gottlieb, Robert, and Peter Wiley
   1984   America's Saints: The Rise of Mormon Power. New York: G. P.
      Putnam's Sons
Gross, F. A.
   1935   Letter to the Commissioner of Indian Affairs, April 11. BIA files,
      Cedar City, Utah.
Gwilliam, Robert F.
   1963   Shivwits Survey. S. Lyman Tyler Papers, Special Collections, Uni-
      versity of Utah.
Hafen, LeRoy, and Ann Hafen, eds.
   1954a   Journals of Forty-Niners: Salt Lake to Los Angeles. Glendale:
      Arthur H. Clark.
   1954b   Old Spanish Trail: Santa Fe to Los Angeles. Glendale: Arthur H.
      Clark.

Hagan, W. T.
1961   American Indians. Chicago: University of Chicago Press.
Hamlin, Jacob
1854–57   Journal of Jacob Hamlin. Manuscript, Utah Historical Society, A567-1. Salt Lake City.
1859   Letter to *The Valley Tan*, February 15.
Hasse, Larry
1974   Termination and Assimilation: Federal Indian Policy 1943–1961. Ph.D. diss., Washington State University.
Haverland, F. M.
1957   Final Report on Paiute Withdrawal in a letter to Commissioner of Indian Affairs, January 3. BIA files, Cedar City, Utah.
Haynes, Alan
1968   The Federal Government and its Policies Regarding the Frontier Era of Utah Territory, 1850–1877. Ph.D. diss., Catholic University of America.
Hill, Leonard M.
1968   Social and Economic Survey of Shivwits, Kanosh, Koosharem, Indian Peaks, and Cedar City Bands of Southern Paiute Indians. BIA files, Cedar City, UT.
Holmes, Graham
1965   Letter to Grant Pete. June 15. BIA files, Cedar City, Utah.
Holmes, Norman
1954a   Report of Meeting at Filmore with Senator Watkins, December 30, 1953. Memorandum to Ralph Gelvin. BIA files, Cedar City, Utah.
1954b   Letter to Alexander Lesser, January 28. BIA files, Cedar City, Utah.
1968   Report to Area Tribal Operations Officer, Phoenix. BIA Files, Cedar City, Utah.
Holt, Ronald L.
1981–90   Paiute Fieldnotes. In Author's possession.
1987   Beneath These Red Cliffs: The Utah Paiutes and Paternalistic Dependency. Ph.D. diss. University of Utah.
1988   The Utah Paiutes and the Indian Claims Commission. Unpublished manuscript in author's possession.
1990   William Palmer and the Paiutes. Unpublished manuscript in author's possession.
Houghton, Ruth, ed.
1973   Native American Politics: Power Relationships in the Western

Great Basin Today. Reno: University of Nevada Bureau of Governmental Research.

Hoxie, Frederrick E.

1984   A Final Promise: The Campaign to Assimilate the Indians, 1880–1920. Lincoln: University of Nebraska Press.

Hunt, Jo Jo

1979   Letter to Mary Ellen Sloan, November 30. M. E. Sloan files. Salt Lake City, Utah.

Indian Claims Commission

1965   Proposed Findings of Fact. John Boyden files. Salt Lake City, Utah.

Inter-Tribal Council of Nevada

1976   Nuwuvi: A Southern Paiute History. Salt Lake City: University of Utah Printing Service.

Irish, O. H.

1865   Articles of Agreement and Convention made and concluded at Pinto Creek. Unratified treaty. National Archives, Record Group 75.

Iron County Record

1924   Article, October 31.

1925   Article, May 15.

1982   Parowan Objects to Paiute Plan. January 14.

Ivins, Anthony

n.d.   Journal in Archives, Church of Jesus Christ of Latter-day Saints, Salt Lake City.

1916   Traveling Over Forgotten Trails. Improvement Era 29: 350–56.

Jacobs, Mary Jane

1974   Termination of Federal Supervision over the Southern Paiute Indians of Utah. M.S. research paper, University of Utah.

Jennings, Jesse D.

1957   Danger Cave. University of Utah Anthropological Papers 27.

Jorgensen, Joseph C.

1972   The Sun Dance Religion. Chicago: University of Chicago Press.

1978   A Century of Political Economic Effects on American Indian Society, 1880–1980. Journal of Ethnic Studies 6: 1–82.

Kanosh Band of Paiute Indians

1951   Minutes of Board Meeting, March 27. BIA files, Cedar City, Utah.

Kelly, Isabel

1934   Southern Paiute Bands. American Anthropologist 36: 548–60.

1939   Southern Paiute Shamanism. Berkeley: University of California Anthropological Records 2: 151–67.

1964   Southern Paiute Ethnography. Salt Lake City: University of Utah Anthropological Papers 69.

Kelley, Isabel, and Cathrine Fowler

1986   Southern Paiute. Pp. 368–97 in Handbook of North American Indians, vol. 11, Great Basin. Ed. by Warren d'Azevedo. Washington, D.C.: Smithsonian Institution.

Kelly, Lawrence

1975   The Indian Reorganization Act: The Dream and the Reality. Pacific Historical Review 44:291–312.

Kleinig, J.

1984   Paternalism. Totowa, N.J.: Rowman and Allenheld.

Knack, Martha

1978   Beyond a Differential: An Inquiry into Southern Paiute Indian Experience with Public Schools. Anthropology and Education Quarterly 9:216–34.

1980   Life is with People: Household Organization of the Contemporary Southern Paiute Indians. Soccoro, N.M.: Ballena Press Anthropological Papers, 19.

1986   On the Processes of Native Adaptation to the Great Basin Ranching Economy. Paper presented at Great Basin Anthropology Conference, Las Vegas, Nevada, October 9–11, 1986.

Laird, Carobeth

1976   The Chemehuevis. Banning, California: Malki Museum Press.

Lamb, Sydney

1958   Linguistic Prehistory of the Great Basin. International Journal of American Linguistics 24:95–100.

Lindblom, Charles E.

1959   The Science of "Muddling Through." Journal of the American Society for Public Administration 19:79–88.

Lonnberg, Allan

1981   The Digger Indian Stereotype in California. Journal of California and Great Basin Anthropology 3:215–23.

Lowie, Robert H.

1924   Notes on Shoshonean Ethnography. American Museum of Natural History Anthropological Papers, 20.

Lurie, Nancy

1957   The Indian Claims Commission Act. Annals of the American Academy of Political and Social Science 311:56–70.

1972   Menominee Termination: From Reservation to Colony. Human Organization 31:257–70.

1978   The Indian Claims Commission. Annals of the American Academy of Political and Social Science 436:97–110.

1985   Epilogue. Pp. 363–82 in Irredeemable America: The Indians' Estate and Land Claims. Ed. by Imre Sutton. Albuquerque: University of New Mexico Press.

MacDonald, Edyth C.

1951   Notes of a Meeting at Cedar City, Richfield and Kanosh, June 5–6, 1951.

Madsen, David

1975   Dating Paiute-Shoshone Expansion in the Great Basin. American Antiquity 40:82–86.

Malouf, Carling, and Arline Malouf

1945   The Effects of Spanish Slavery on the Intermountain West. Southwestern Journal of Anthropology 1:378–91.

Manning, William

n.d.   My Work among the Indians. Unpublished manuscript. Copy in Ronald Holt files. Layton, Utah.

Martineau, J.

1855   Letter to George A. Smith, Deseret News, July 11.

Mauss, Marcel

1954   The Gift: Forms and Functions of Exchange in Archaic Societies. Glencoe, Ill.: The Free Press.

McConihe, W. W.

1915   Report to Lorenzo Creel, October 19. Scattered Bands, National Archives, Record Group 75.

Meese, Edwin

1983   Letter to Name Withheld, August 29, 1983. M. E. Sloan files. Salt Lake City, Utah.

Mehojah, W. A.

1975   Memorandum to files. February 14, 1975. BIA files, Cedar City, Utah.

Meriam, Lewis, ed.

1928   The Problem of Indian Administration. Baltimore: Johns Hopkins Press.

Miller, Wick

1986   Numic Languages. Pp. 98–106 in Handbook of North American Indians, vol. 11, Great Basin. Ed. by Warren d'Azevedo. Washington: Smithsonian Institution.

Milner, Clyde

1982   With Good Intentions: Quaker Work among the Pawnees, Otos, and Omahas in the 1870s. Lincoln: University of Nebraska Press.

Milner, Clyde, and Floyd O'Neil, eds.

1985   Churchmen and the Western Indians 1820–1920. Norman: University of Oklahoma Press.

Mintz, Sidney

1977   The So-Called World System: Local Initiative and Local Response. Dialectical Anthropology 2:253–70.

Morgan, Dale

1987   The State of Deseret. Logan: Utah State University.

Myer, Dillon

1952   Withdrawal Memorandum, August 6, 1952.

Nash, June

1981   Ethnographic Aspects of the World Capitalist System. Annual Review of Anthropology 10:393–423.

Nielsen, Richard A.

1973   American Indian Land Claims: Land versus Money as a Remedy. University of Florida Law Review 25:308–26.

O'Dea, Thomas

1957   The Mormons. Chicago: University of Chicago Press.

Olson, James S., and Raymond Wilson

1984   Native Americans in the Twentieth Century. Urbana and Chicago: University of Illincis Press.

Orfield, Gary

1965   A Study of the Termination Policy. Denver: National Congress of American Indians.

1983   Termination, Destruction and Restoration. Indian Self-Rule: Fifty Years under the Indian Reorganization Act. Sun Valley, Idaho: Institute of the American West.

Owens, Nancy

1976   Indian Reservations and Bordertowns: The Metropolis-Satellite Model Applied to the Northeastern Navahos and the Umatillas. Ph.D. diss., University of Oregon.

Paiute Indian Tribe of Utah

1981   Tribal Council Minutes, October 24.

1982   Proposed Paiute Indian Tribe of Utah Reservation Plan (draft). Cedar City: Paiute Tribe.

1983   Paiute Department of Education Report May 28. Copy in Ronald Holt files, Layton, Utah.

Paiute Indian Tribe of Utah Newsletter

1984   Newsletter No. 41. March 19.

1984   Newsletter No. 43. April 19.

1984   Newsletter No. 51. September 21.

1985   Newsletter No. 69. September 30.

Palmer, William R.

1929   Pahute Indian Government and Laws. Utah Historical Quarterly 2:35–42.

1933   Pahute Indian Homelands. Utah Historical Quarterly 6:88–103.

1936a   Journal (untitled). Unpublished manuscript, Special Collections, Southern Utah State College, Cedar City, Utah.

1936b   The Religion of the Piutes. Improvement Era September 1936. Vol 39:539, 534–576.

1942   Pahute Indian Medicine. Manuscript. Special Collections. Southern Utah State College, Cedar City, Utah.

1946a   The Wahnquint Indians. Unpublished manuscript, Special Collections, Southern Utah State College, Cedar City, Utah.

1946b   Letter to Ernest L. Wilkinson, December 31. Special Collections, Southern Utah State College, Cedar City, Utah.

1946c   Report on Indian Affairs. Special Collections, Southern Utah State College, Cedar City, Utah.

Parry, Bruce

1975   Memo to Chairmen, Paiute Bands, March 12. Copy in Ronald Holt files. Layton, Utah.

n.d.   Letter to John Artichoker [1975].

Pendergast, David, and Clement Meighan

1959   Folk Traditions as Historical Fact: A Paiute Example. Journal of American Folklore 72:128–33.

Peroff, Nicholas

1982   Menominee Drums: Tribal Termination and Restoration, 1954–74. Norman: University of Oklahoma Press.

Pete, Woodrow, et al.

1968   Letter to Deseret News, June 5.

Peterson, Charles S.

1975   Jacob Hamblin, Apostle to the Lamanites, and the Indian Mission. Journal of Mormon History 2:21–34.

Petersen, Mark

1981   Children of Promise. Salt Lake City: Bookcraft.

Petition of Contract Attorneys

n.d.   [1965?] John Boyden files. Salt Lake City, Utah.

Philp, Kenneth R., ed.

1977 John Collier's Crusade for Indian Reform, 1920–45. Tuscon: University of Arizona Press.

1983 Termination: A Legacy of the Indian New Deal. Western Historical Quarterly 14: 165–80.

1986 Indian Self-Rule. Salt Lake City: Howe Brothers.

Pierce, Margaret H.

1977 The Work of the Indian Claims Commission. American Bar Association Journal 63:227–32.

Powell, Charles

1871 Letter to H. R. Clum. Annual Report of the Commissioner of Indian Affairs, 1871, Serial Set 1565, pp. 561–62.

Powell, J. W., and G. W. Engalls

1874 U.S. Special Commission, Report on the Condition of the Ute Indians of Utah; the Pai-Utes of Utah etc. Annual Report of the Commissioner of Indian Affairs, Serial Set 1601, 1873.

Prucha, Francis

1984 The Great Father, The U.S. Government and the Indians. 2 vols. Lincoln: University of Nebraska Press.

1986 The Great Father, abridged ed. Lincoln: University of Nebraska Press.

Ragsdale, Pat

1979 Letter to Commissioner of Indian Affairs, September 13. BIA files, Cedar City, Utah.

Realty Officer [Frank Scott?]

1956 Letter to William Fitzpatrick, December 17. BIA files, Cedar City, Utah.

1957 Letter to Area Director, August 7. BIA files, Cedar City, Utah.

Rembar, Charles

1980 The Law of the Land. New York: Simon and Schuster.

Richfield Reaper

1983 Dan Marriott's Pipe Dream Doesn't Serve Anyone. April 20.

Rosenthal, Harvey D.

1985 Indian Claims and the American Conscience: A Brief History of the Indian Claims Commission. Pp. 35–70 in Irredeemable America: The Indians' Estate and Land Claims. Ed. by Imre Sutton. Albuquerque: University of New Mexico Press.

Sale, Thomas

1865 Letter to O. H. Irish, May 4. Annual Report of the Commissioner of Indian Affairs, 1865, Serial Set 1248, p. 155.

Salt Lake Tribune

   1981   Paiute Finally Regaining Status, Self-Sufficiency, September 20.

   1982   Paiute Hope to Gain U.S. Acreage, February 15.

Sapir, Edward

   1910   Southern Paiute Fieldnotes, American Philosophical Library, Philadelphia. Copy in Ronald Holt files. Layton, Utah.

   1930–31   Southern Paiute, A Shoshonean Language. Proceedings of the American Academy of Arts and Sciences, 65.

Sartorius, Rolf, ed.

   1983   Paternalism. Minneapolis: University of Minnesota Press.

Schusky, Ernest L.

   1979   Political Constraints of Economic Development: The Dakota Reservations. Pp. 337–62 in Currents in Anthropology: Essays in Honor of Sol Tax. Ed. by Robert Hinshaw. The Hague: Mouton.

Scott, Frank

   1956a   Action Taken Report. BIA files, Cedar City, Utah.

   1956b   Final Termination Report [November 14, 1956]. BIA files, Cedar City, Utah.

   1957   Letter to George McFee, April 26. BIA files, Cedar City, Utah.

Service, Elman

   1955   Indian-European Relations in Colonial Latin America. American Anthropologist 57:411–25.

Shapard, John

   1964   Brief Summaries of (7) Seven Tribal Meetings. BIA Files, Cedar City, Utah.

Sheehan, Bernard W.

   1973   Seeds of Extinction: Jeffersonian Philanthropy and the American Indian. New York: W. W. Norton.

Simpson, J. H.

   1869   The Shortest Route to California. Philadelphia: J. B. Lippincott.

Sloan, Mary Ellen

   n.d.   Restoration Chronology. Unpublished manuscript drawn from the files of Mary Ellen Sloan and Larry Echohawk. Salt Lake City, Utah.

Smith, Carol

   1978   Beyond Dependency Theory: National and Regional Patterns of Underdevelopment in Guatemala. American Ethnologist 5(2):574–617.

   1983   Regional Analysis in World-System Perspective: A Critique of Three Structural Theories of Uneven Development. Pp. 307–59 in Economic Anthropology. Ed. by Sutti Ortiz. Lantham, Md.: University Press of America.

Smith, M. G.

1966   A Structural Approach to Comparative Politics. Pp. 113–28 in Varieties of Political Theory. Ed. by David Easton. Englewood Cliffs: Prentice-Hall.

Snow, William

1929   Utah Indians and the Spanish Slave Trade. Utah Historical Quarterly 2:67–90.

Social Science Research Council

1954   Acculturation: An Exploratory Formulation. American Anthropologist 56:973–1002.

Sorensen Lease Agreement

1969   Copy in Ronald Holt files. Layton, Utah.

Spencer, Anne

1973   Cultural Value Systems in Southern Utah. Boulder: Western Interstate Commission for Higher Education.

Spicer, Edward H.

1961   Cycles of Conquest. Tucson: University of Arizona Press.

1971   Persistent Cultural Systems. Science 174:795–800.

Spier, Leslie

1928   Havasupai Ethnography. New York: Anthropological Papers of the American Museum of Natural History 29:81–392.

Spindler, G. D.

1955   Sociocultural and Psychological Processes in Menomini Acculturation. Publications in Culture and Society, vol. 5. Berkeley: University of California Press.

Stevens, Harry

1954   Letter to Rex Lee, October 22. BIA files, Cedar City, Utah.

Steward, Julian

1938   Basin-Plateau Aboriginal Sociopolitical Groups, 1970 reprint ed. Salt Lake City: University of Utah Press.

1955a   Southern Paiute Bands. Unpublished paper in file of Southern Paiute Litigation Case, 1955. Papers of Julian Steward, Box 12. Archives, University of Illinois at Urbana-Champaign.

1955b   Letter to Ralph Barney, December 17. Papers of Julian Steward, Box 12. Archives, University of Illinois at Urbana-Champaign.

1970   The Foundations of Basin-Plateau Shoshonean Society. Pp. 113–51 in Languages and Cultures of Western North America. Ed. by Earl

Swanson. Pocatello, Idaho: Idaho State University Press.

Stewart, Jon, and Peter Wiley
1981   Cultural Genocide. Penthouse (June):81–164.

Stewart, Omer C.
1942   Culture Element Distributions XVIII: Ute-Southern Paiute. University of California Anthropological Records 6:231–355.
1961   Kroeber and the Indian Claims Commission Cases. Kroeber Anthropological Society Papers 25:181–90.

Stoffle, Richard, and Henry Dobyns
1982   Puaxantu Tuvip. Kenosha: University of Wisconsin-Parkside.

Stoffle, Richard; Henry Dobyns; and Michael Evans
1983   Nungwu-Uakapi: Southern Paiute Indians Comment on the Intermountain Power Project. Kenosha, Wis.: University of Wisconsin-Parkside.

Stoffle, Richard, and Michael Evans
1976   Resource Competition and Population Change: A Kaibab Paiute Ethnohistorical Case. Ethnohistory 23:173–97.

Stone, Forrest
1951a   Letter to P. Church. March 22. Denver FRC, Group 75.
1951b   Letter to Commissioner of Indian Affairs. July 10. Denver Federal Records Center Group 75.

Taylor, Graham D.
1980   The New Deal and American Indian Tribalism. Lincoln: University of Nebraska Press.

Thomas, Robert K.
1966/67   Colonialism: Classic and Internal. New University Thought 4:37–44.

Thompson, Gregory C.
1983   Representative Reva Beck Bosone, Senator Arthur V. Watkins and the Framing of Tribal Termination. Paper presented to the Western History Conference, October 14, 1983, Salt Lake City, Utah.

Trimberger, Ellen Kay
1979   World Systems Analysis: The Problem of Unequal Development. Theory and Society 8:127–37.

Tyler, S. Lyman
1964   A Work Paper on Termination: With an Attempt to Show its Antecedents. Provo, Utah: Institute of American Indian Studies.
1973   A History of Indian Policy. Washington, D.C.: U.S. Government Printing Office.

Underdal, S. J.

1977   On the Road toward Termination: The Pyramid Lake Paiutes and the Indian Attorney Controversy of the 1950s. Ph.D. diss., Columbia University.

U.S. Bureau of Indian Affairs

1899   Annual Report of the CIA. Denver Federal Records Center, Group 75.

1917   Annual Report, Superintendent of the Paiute Goshute Agency, to the Commissioner of Indian Affairs. National Archives, Federal Records Group 75.

1918–1919   Annual Report of the Paiute Goshute Agency to the Commissioner of Indian Affairs. Denver Federal Records Center, Group 72.

1931   Annual Report of the Board of Indian Commissioners. National Archives, Federal Records Group 75.

1932–1936   Annual Narrative Reports, Denver Federal Records Center, Group 75.

1936   Indian Reorganization Committee. Findings and Recommendations, September 30, 1936. Denver Federal Records Center, Group 75.

1946   Plan of Operations: Shivwits Agriculture, Livestock and Range Enterprise. BIA files, Cedar City, Utah.

1952a   Draft of Withdrawal Status. BIA files, Cedar City, Utah.

1952b   Summary Statement of Withdrawal Status, June 30. BIA files, Cedar City, Utah.

1953   Final Report of Withdrawal Staff. BIA files, Cedar City, Utah.

1954   BIA Report of January 28. BIA files, Cedar City, Utah.

1955   Contract No. 14-20-450-552 between the United States and the University of Utah for the Education of Adult Indians, July 1.

1956   Withdrawal Program Coordinating Staff to Commissioner of Indian Affairs, July 23. BIA files, Cedar City, Utah.

1957   Trusteeship Account. BIA files, Cedar City, Utah.

1957   Trusteeship Account Ledger, Indian Peaks Band of Paiute Indians. BIA files, Cedar City, Utah.

1971   Apportionment and Disposition of Funds Awarded Southern Utah Paiute Nation, BIA Files, Cedar City, Utah.

1982   Development Potential for Shivwits Indian Reservation. BIA files, Cedar City, Utah.

U.S. Congress

1954   Termination of Federal Supervision over Certain Tribes of Indians, Joint Hearings on S. 2670 and H. 7674 before the Subcommittees of the Committees on Interior and Insular Affairs, 83rd

Congress, 2nd Session. Washington, D.C.: U.S. Government Printing Office.

U.S. House of Representatives
   1945   House Committee on Indian Affairs
   Hearings on H.R. 1198 and H.R. 1341. 79th Congress, 1st Session. Washington, D.C.: U.S. Government Printing Office.
   1984   Interior Appropriations Committee
   Testimony, February 21. Washington, D.C.: U.S. Government Printing Office.

U.S. Senate
   1954   Senator Watkins, 83d Cong., 2d sess., May 4, Congressional Record, vol. 100:5926
   1983   Senate Select Committee on Indian Affairs Trust Lands for the Paiute Tribe of Utah. Hearing held Nov. 2, 1983. Senate hearing 98-590. Washington, D.C.: U.S. Government Printing Office.

Utah State Board of Indian Affairs
   1974   Meeting minutes. February 6.
   1975   Meeting minutes. May 15.

Vance, John T.
   1969   The Congressional Mandate and the Indian Claims Commission. North Dakota Law Review 45:325–36.

Van den Berghe, Pierre
   1985   Comment. Current Anthropology 26:262–63.

VanDeVeer, Donald
   1986   Paternalistic Intervention: The Moral Bounds on Benevolence. Princeton: Princeton University Press.

Vincent, Joan
   1978   Political Anthropology: Manipulative Strategies. Annual Review of Anthropology 7:175–94.

Vogel, Dan
   1986   Indian Origins and the Book of Mormon. Salt Lake City: Signature Books.

Wagner, Charles
   1915   Letter to Commissioner of Indian Affairs, Denver Federal Records Center, Group 75.

Wallerstein, Immanuel
   1974   The Modern World System: Capitalist Agriculture and the Origins of the European World-Economy in the Sixteenth Century. New York: Academic Press.

1979   The Capitalist World Economy. London: Cambridge University Press.

Warner, Ted, ed.
1976   The Domínguez-Escalante Journal. Provo: BYU Press.

Washington County [Utah] Welfare
1961   The November 17 Problem. BIA files, Cedar City, Utah.
1962   Welfare Report. BIA files, Cedar City, Utah.

Watkins, Arthur
1949   Letter to William Palmer, February 1. Palmer files, Special Collections, Southern Utah State College, Cedar City.
1957   Termination of Federal Supervision: The Removal of Restrictions over Indian Property and Person. Annals of the American Academy of Political and Social Sciences 311:47–55.

Weissbrodt, I. S., and John Boyden
1965   Petition of Contract Attorneys for Award of Attorney Fees and Statement in Support of Petition for Allowance of Attorney Fees. John Boyden files. Salt Lake City, Utah.

White, J. E.
1946a   Social and Economic Information of the Kanosh Band of Paiute Indians, March 1946. BIA files, Cedar City, Utah.
1946b   Social and Economic Information of the Shivwits Band of Paiute Indians, June 1946. BIA files, Cedar City, Utah.

White, John R.
1978   Barmecide Revisited: The Gratuitous Offset in Indian Claims Cases. Ethnohistory 25/2:179–92.

White, Leslie
1949   The Science of Culture. New York: Grove Press.

White, Richard
1983   The Roots of Dependency. Lincoln: University of Nebraska Press.

Whittaker, David J.
1985   Mormons and Native Americans: A Historical and Bibliographical Introduction. Dialogue 18:33–64.

Wilcox, Dee
1975   Letter to Superintendent of Unitah and Ouray Reservation, March 17. Denver Federal Records Center, RG 75.

Wiley, Peter, and Robert Gottlieb
1982   Empires in the Sun. Tucson: University of Arizona Press.

Wilkinson, Charles, and Eric Briggs
1977   The Evolution of the Termination Policy. American Indian Law Review 5:139–84.

Wilkinson, Cragun and Barker
  1954 Memorandum to Senator Arthur Watkins, February 23. John Boy-
         den files. Salt Lake City, Utah.
Wilkinson, Ernest L.
  1955 Letter to Carl Hawkins, January 11. Copy in Ronald Holt files.
         Layton, Utah.
Wilkinson, Ernest L., and Leonard Arrington
  1976 Brigham Young University: The First One Hundred Years. Provo:
         BYU Press.
Wilkinson, Glen A.
  1955 Memorandum for Ernest L. Wilkinson, February 14. Wilkinson
         files, BYU.
  1966 Indian Tribal Claims Before the Court of Claims. Georgetown Law
         Journal 55:511–28.
Winkler, Albert
  1987 The Circleville Massacre: A Brutal Incident in Utah's Black Hawk
         War. Utah Historical Quarterly 55:4–21.
Withdrawal Program Coordinating Staff
  1956 Report to BIA, July 23, 1956. BIA files, Cedar City, Utah.
Witherspoon, Y. T.
  1955 Interim Report for the Educational-Vocational Survey of the Ute,
         Kanosh, Koosharem, Indian Peaks, and Shivwit Indians. Salt Lake City:
         Extension Division, University of Utah.
Wolf, Eric
  1982 Europe and the People without History. Berkeley: University of
         California Press.
Woodbury, Angus
  1944 A History of Southern Utah and its National Parks. Utah Historical
         Quarterly 12:111–209.
Woolsey, Nethella
  1964 The Escalante Story. Springville, Utah: Art City Publishing.
Work, Laura
  1899 Report of Shebits Day School, at St. George, Utah. Annual Reports
         of the Department of the Interior.
  1917 Annual Report. U.S. Department of the Interior. National Ar-
         chives, Federal Records Group 75.
Worthman, Charles
  1972 Letter to Joy Leland. BIA files, Cedar City, Utah.

INDEX